A. K. Ramanujan
Poems and a Novella

Books in English by A. K. Ramanujan

Poetry

The Striders (1966)

Relations (1971)

Selected Poems (1976)

Second Sight (1986)

Collected Poems (1995)

The Oxford India Ramanujan (2004)

Translations

The Interior Landscape: Love Poems from a Classical Tamil Anthology (1967)

Speaking of Siva, Kannada vacana poems by Virasaiva saints (1973)

Samskara: A Rite for a Dead Man, a Kannada novel by U. R. Anantha Murthy (1976)

Hymns for the Drowning: Poems for Visnu by Nammalvar and the Ten Long Poems of Classical Tamil (1985)

Folktales from India: A Selection of Oral Tales from Twenty-two Languages (1991)

Co-authored and Co-edited Books

The Literature of India: An Introduction (1974), with Edward Dimock Jr. and others

Another Harmony: New Essays on the Folklore of India (1986), with Stuart Blackburn

When God is a Customer: Telugu Courtesan Songs by Ksetrayya and Others (posthumous, 1994), with V. Narayana Rao and David Shulman

The Oxford Anthology of Modern Indian Poetry (posthumous, 1994), with Vinay Dharwadker

Posthumous

The Black Hen in *Collected Poems* (1995)

The Flowering Tree and Other Oral Tales from India (1997)

Collected Essays (1999)

Uncollected Poems and Prose (2000)

Oxford India Ramanujan (2004)

A. K. Ramanujan
Poems and a Novella

Translated from Kannada
by

Tonse N. K. Raju
AND
Shouri Daniels-Ramanujan

Advisory Editor
Prithvi Datta Chandra Shobhi

OXFORD
UNIVERSITY PRESS

OXFORD
UNIVERSITY PRESS

YMCA Library Building, Jai Singh Road, New Delhi 110 001

Oxford University Press is a department of the University of Oxford.
It furthers the University's objective of excellence in research, scholarship,
and education by publishing worldwide in

Oxford   New York

Auckland   Cape Town   Dar es Salaam   Hong Kong   Karachi
Kuala Lumpur   Madrid   Melbourne   Mexico City   Nairobi
New Delhi   Shanghai   Taipei   Toronto

With offices in

Argentina   Austria   Brazil   Chile   Czech Republic   France   Greece
Guatemala   Hungary   Italy   Japan   Poland   Portugal   Singapore
South Korea   Switzerland   Thailand   Turkey   Ukraine   Vietnam

Oxford is a registered trademark of Oxford University Press
in the UK and in certain other countries.

Published in India
by Oxford University Press, New Delhi

ISBN-13: 978-0-19-567498-9
ISBN-10: 0-19-567498-7

Typeset in Lapidary333 BT 12/14.5
by Eleven Arts, Keshav Puram, Delhi 110 035
Printed in India by Rashtriya Printer, New Delhi 110 032
Published by Manzar Khan, Oxford University Press
YMCA Library Building, Jai Singh Road, New Delhi 110 001

Acknowledgements

I invited Ramanujan's friend, Krishna Raju, to be the co-translator of this book three years ago. He had moved from Chicago to Washington D.C. Within weeks, he was sending to me in Northfield by email the Kannada novella, *Someone Else's Autobiography (SEA)*, a chapter at a time. Later, he emailed each of the Kannada poems, word-for-word, phrase-by-phrase, line-by-line. On receiving each page, I would try to decipher what he sent me; the results were sent back and forth, several times. Some of the poems were vexed/vexing, slippery, requiring endurance from the translators, as the poems stubbornly refused to go obediently into English. Finally, when we had done a working draft, I sent them to Prithvi Datta Chandra Shobhi in Chicago. As advisory editor, Prithvi pointed out our errors and misses. Each time, I rewrote a passage or line, I would send a copy first to Krishna Raju, and if he concurred, I would forward the pages to Prithvi. This went on till all three of us found the result satisfactory. Prithvi and Krishna Raju read each draft at the highest level. If I feel confident about the merit of this volume, it is because of their extraordinary loyalty to Ramanujan's texts. Along the way, each of us has accumulated our share of debts to those who helped us.

Krishna Raju acknowledges the helpful discussions he had with Dr Siva Subramanian and Vikas Kamat; he is grateful to T. N. Raghupathy for finding English equivalents for the Iyengar argot in *SEA*; he would most like to thank his wife Vidya, and sons, Sharat and Manu, who each went over the text.

Prithvi Datta Chandra Shobhi would like to acknowledge help

from Manu Shetty, particularly about the second to last poem in *Kuntobille*, 'Marana Sarana'.

To these debts, I must add my own. I am grateful to: Krittika Ramanujan for the use of the etching, *Portrait of Father*; Somanahalli Diwakar for reading the first 12 pages of *SEA* and encouraging us to push on; Connie Rew for being a first reader of *SEA*; Ricky and David Peterson for being our poetry readers; Bronwen Bledsoe for putting me in touch with Prithvi Shobhi and for reading the proofs, and I am most grateful to Kanishka G. B. Marasinghe for reading the final proofs; Krittika and Krishna Ramanujan for their ongoing help as literary consultants, and finally Mark Heiman for help in designing the covers for *Uncollected Poems and Prose, The Oxford India Ramanujan*, and this one.

All of us are grateful to A. K. Ramanujan for challenging us with passages that resisted easy access, and for his characteristic use of irony.

Shouri Daniels-Ramanujan
Northfield, September 2005

Editor's Note

For readers of English poetry who are unfamiliar with Indian mythology, literature, rituals, sources, and allusions: glosses and notes are provided at the end of the book. The notes will help readers who are new to Ramanujan's poems, translations, and essays.

Contents

BOOK TWO: A NOVELLA

Book One: Poems

Part 1: No Lotus in the Navel

Part 2: And Other Poems

Part 3: Kuntobille

PART 1

No Lotus in the Navel

by

A. K. RAMANUJAN

CONTENTS

A King of Soliloquies

Before we finished talking, my neck
grew a ganglion of cancer cells
    I tried to find a voice
    for the voiceless, whose
    equine grins were dis-
    regarded by tacit nurses.
I tried to speak for them
I found my throat was blocked.

Before we finished talking, my illiterate
Love, whose letters were written by me,
    who inspired a closet full of stories
    and poems, and has given me all heartache,
    was wed, the very hour I received
    the Kannada Association's award
in the month of Mithuna,[†] the month
of love, and I played Onan to my fist.

Before we finished talking, a stench rose
from corpses, their snuffed eyes wide open.
    I wished to be their voice
    I opened my mouth to speak and
    people, indifferent to the havoc
    of napalm in Vietnam, said,
pinching their noses in the air—Phew! Your
mouth reeks far worse than carrion.

Before we finished talking, I desired
to find the voice trapped in me
    I wanted to give utterance
    to what I had seen,
    observations noted, but those
    in high chairs found me boring.
They fled, and I dropped miles away into
a back street, to become the king of soliloquies.

The Month of Fire (*Agni Masa*)

In a crowless month
   in a month of fire
   in the half-light of
a screened verandah

the bangles on a gypsy
   hand flashed points
 of light, and I said,
Do not enter! Be gone!

A Meditation on Doors

Here, when a door is shut
And the latch is in place
People get suspicious.
There, doors pull shut
As if pushed by wind.

Sensors open doors to visitors
Caught together in a revolving
Door; my wife's long nose
Presses against my shoulder blade
And fingers do the dialling
To signal, 'Open Sesame', past
The bronze-handled bank door.

Here, houses have thresholds
Without doors. When Atthe's
Third daughter-in-law 'needed to go'
She was pregnant and the whole village came.
They broke open a door. She gave birth
To her first son, now in Bengal, an engineer.
The door is a dwarake,[†] like Lord Krishna's birthplace
From ages ago; temple doors close at midnight
Bells chime with blown breezes and doors fly open
For the tribhanga[†] gods. Having gone to the temple
At 8:30, mother said, 'Why do they shut the doors
At 8:00? Do they fear thieves even in a temple?'

Doors become walls when shut;
Walls become doors when open
And those outside are in,
But when a door closes
There is east and west,

A. K. RAMANUJAN

North, south, inside and outside.
Even a god hanging from a nail
Gets claustrophobic from walls.
A noose of fear can hang
From a beam. The dangling Hindi
Film star is not doing the eighth
Position in the *Kama Sutra*.†

If the door is open, there are people.
If shut, there are rumours and
Turmoil in the navel.
If the door is open to the wind
Beyond the palms, and to the gossip
Of the day—about the quarrel
Of a couple after dinner; about
What could happen if he left
For Vietnam; about how the boy
Who dropped the bicycle was caught
That day; about the palm tree possessed
By a demon; about how a wind-filled
Sari began to be seen as being pregnant.

A wall sports many doors and windows.
A door needs just one wall.
Half-built houses get their light from the sky.
Think of a field and a solitary threshold
Standing alone, think then of a window
That has no memory of bars;
Look for a blue map of doors and look
Again for a fresh hidden door; find
The handle made of fresh wood, and smell
The sawdust and lumber lying around
From felled trees; then consider doors that
Are not doors that can and cannot not be.

Connections

1

Poets of a certain ilk
Find poems in imagined worlds.
Seers with a certain
Cast of mind
Catch the light from darkest days;
They write Radha-Krishna† love songs.

2

Study it long enough: a dark blot
Becomes a donkey's ears, stretched out;
Flaking cement skin, a carbuncular face,
The ridge of a broken nose,
Or another view of Karma;
Same as when a grain of sand
Shows up in the X-ray of a pearl,
Same as when a sculptor's compass
Leaves its angle on a dancer's leg,
Same as when, behind the eyes of seers,
The wind may move the silken
Weavings of a white sari—such poets go
Sniffing around the feet of strangers,
Even if their hands are
Paralysed by forbidden fires.

3

Under banks of clouds, unobserved,
A bull roams the village street;

Red sampige† flowers trail
The walls, and as on a lighted
Screen, see a broken-down car, a leaky tap,
And see the dishpan with bits of rice.

4

Sophia Church has forty stained
Glass windows. The sunlight
Blushes every girl and every boy
Who comes to worship in the church.
Blue-green, sea-green, yellow of gold
Purple, vermilion, grey and brown,

And in the rotunda of the dome
A wheel of pantheonic gods
And others, shower each worshipper,
A pentimento of changing colours
Charged with sentimental lore,
Their eyes reflecting seven colours.

Inside the Hanumanta† temple,
There are never any windows.
In the darkness of the shrine room
The priest moves a camphor flame
In circles, throwing shadows
Of circumambulating worshippers
Enlarged as in a shadow play
Circling across the granite walls:
Pillars of stone, and long canine teeth
Of demons, guarding entrances
And then, the tall lamp's single flame reveals
A shadow with forty heads on a single body.

5

At Maharaj Jai Singh's observatory
The Jantar Mantar† in New Delhi
A saw-toothed wheel measures Time's
Footprints between sun and earth,
And chariot wheels of the sun god, minute by minute,
Run Time's ever-silent sunday horse race.

Arches and pillars throw changing
Shadows on the ground. Noon's stunted Vamana†
Rises to evening's gigantic Trivikrama,†
Changing again at night into a giant third step.
Walking in place all night on terra firma, yet covering
The skies. Tall grasses grow and mulch around his toes.

6

The goddess of poetry
Desires to take bodily form.
The mandala† of earth carries
Sun's warmth to the hidden moon,
To the quarter moon, to the harvest moon,
Between Rahu and Ketu,† between the bellows
Of the gods and the moulting, planet-
Gobbling demon snake, the eternal rope.

7

Wouldn't you say,
This is getting to be a bit much?
Think: when hair falls from the scalp
The shadow too disappears; then look
For the light downy hair that is not gray.

Some Days

if he were to stumble
at the corner of the house
he might injure
his spine;

some days
if he were to dig up
the vegetable patch,
he might find
ancestral bones;

some days
even if he were to repeat
Agasthya's mantra,
'Vatapi be digested!'[†]
his belly might still
burst open;

some days
even if rain could
wash away stains,
blood might bubble
up in eyes,

like
the bombed-out red
womb of a mother
on the morning of her
daughter's birth,

like
the red dew, inside
the black kanigele[†] flower,
carrying sugar and salt
at dawn.

A Father's Gift

Father bought a child's
umbrella and a watch for me.

He (six feet tall and three
extra feet of umbrella held aloft
next to me who was three feet tall)
turned me into a soggy midget.

By his side, I would get splashed
on the left side when going and on the right
side when returning, and with each step
of his flipflops he would spray me more
and even when the rain stopped, the rim
of his umbrella would drip on me.

Out of pity, my giant would walk bent over
looking every bit like a hunchbacked dwarf
and I would be overcome with laughter
and if he folded up his umbrella, its wayward
ribs would threaten to gouge my eyes
rip my nose and pierce my neck. I tell you
it was no easy matter to be under a father's
umbrella, and so he bought one for me.

He threw in a watch for good measure
and we walked companionably in the rain
each with his own umbrella till my brother
ruined the ribs of mine while fencing with it
and during Sunday's storm the ribs turned
convex; the watch too stopped within a week.

I crushed my watch in the mortar Grandmother
used for pounding supari;† mother spanked me
and for days, she cleaned the springs of the watch.

When grandmother ground sour supari balls
my two-teeth grandmother would say, 'Why Ramu,
Are the teeth of your watch being ground for me?'

On Blast-off and Re-entry

As astronauts:
  While ascending, do we carry
  our everyday fear, our body's
  waste, our hunger for rice
  and the everyday surprises
  of our animal blood?
As astronauts:
  Inside the machine
  charged by a calculator
  at countdown to zero and blast-off,
  we shoot through the umbilicus
  of Mother Earth leaving behind
  air and light, into a void,
  circumnavigating ten times,
  pumping away, we see our
  earth as a moon, we see what
  we earthlings, under the blue coverlid,
  have never seen. Africa is divided
  by night and light: day lights up
  the southern half; the darkness
  of night is on the face of the north;
  the moon's lovely face is pitted;
  we observe what was once imagined.
  We glimpse the visvarupa†
  or form of the cosmos.
  We take pictures for posterity.
As astronauts:
  We return to earth, wind, and water,
  to our dogs, and the electric light,
  wondering: where on earth are we?

We count to zero and on re-entry,
upside down, our gravity returns;
we splashdown into a lake,
to body's hunger, body's waste,
the smell of the street, the unfamiliar
shift from night to alternating day,
primed and wound like watches
we are back in the mohullas†
of our everyday lives, our
streets and our houses.

And Now at Midnight

As Arjuna,[†]
disguised as a eunuch
dancing master, spoke,

Fear abated
and like me, Uttara,[†]
the timorous crown prince
who has never hunted anything larger
than ants, gnats, or butterflies,
grew new hair on the chest
(and becoming emboldened)
wanted to hunt cheetahs at night
even as Arjuna's
divine bow[†] shot
an arrow to start
a conflagration
that licked the ground
of the Khandava[†] forest.

And see now at midnight
in the twisting cobbled street
of the old city of Mysore
under petromax lamps
our lowly tonga-wallah[†]
no longer the horse-gram-
belching coin-juggling
chappie of the ordinary day
become the great warrior
in a horse-shoe-gleaming gallop
to the sound of trumpets

in a cloud of dust, rising
above the ramparts, and see
Uttara's face shining
in the heat of strobe lights.

On the Bathroom Sink

A full set
   of teeth
      smiled at
         me generously.
           Appa's
       forgotten
    new set
  of dentures,
I realized.

Arjuna Looks at Draupadi
during the Year of Their Disguise

Go, my words, go quickly and find
her flawless jasmine-scented self.

Go, cup her face between your palms
And kiss her on the mouth.

Go, stroke that ruby red palace
With your finger tip and reach

Her parted hair and let it down.
Go, reach her voice as clear

As a tinkling bell. Go, feel her modest
Zone and the dark cleavage of kama[†]

Below her sloping underbelly,
The downy bush in her night's

Sari and feel each day and night
Her fullness. Go, spread her limbs;

Tame them, pluck the stars and
Scatter them in the path of enemies.

Go, send floral arrows to Draupadi.
I, Bruhannale, can only speak to her who

Can open the floodgates
And light my *jyotirlingam*.[†]

American Ladybug

Maytide
   Springtide
Red-lacquered
   Ladybug with
Five black dots like
   Liquorice seeds
A sixth dot on
   the head—two eyes
And a one-hair feeler
   To taste the world

America-made
   Ladybug
Mother bug
   Baby bug
Needing food
   Needing sleep
Fed by fear
   Of fire
Feeling thirst
   Hunger for mating
A six-legged hero
   To amoebas
A behemoth
   To mosquitoes

Bug perching
    On the whorl
Of my thumbprint
    Fluttering away
With dust motes
    Whirring
Inaudibly
    A grubtime
Bell to waiting
    Chirping sparrows.

A. K. RAMANUJAN

In Madhurai

the city of temples,
a half-nosed dented face
fingers and heels eaten up,
eyes prurient, plagued by
the persistence of mosquitoes,
this lazar-leper with iridescent
flies on nagamuri[†] flowers
has by him, his attendant wife
sporting a new wedding tali[†]
at the entrance to the ancient
temple, he stands

against the bas-relief
of apsaras,[†] heavenly nymphs
carved by hand, on the door
of the temple, their lips curving
in a smile prescribed in the thirty-second
verse of the *Shilpa Shastra*,[†]
their noses broken,

and the razed tribhanga[†] pose
of body, bent to music in dance,
holding the prescribed posture—
even though wrecked by Khilji's[†]
grandson—and again, the figleaf
medallion with the Sanskrit
inscription on it, destroyed
by Tamil zealots, more recently:

all these went into my lecture
on life and art, which was
well received in America.

Similitudes

a house
in the middle of the forest

grass sprouting
in the cracks of cinder blocks

cilantro
in an American market.

One of the Five Bhutas†

Place of shanti†
 Place of peace
Place of lotus pads, algae, cholera bacilli
 River of death, river of life
River of human waste to one side;
 Bath suds from women
Washing on days of the curse
 On the other side.

River of swift currents
 River of detachment
River of abundance
 How can I drink this water?
Outside our city
 Municipal engineers designed
A reservoir sterilizing and filtering
 The panchagavya.†

They give us treated water three hours
 Each day, through gridwork
Of pipes and conduits.
 The water is bitter to the taste now
And during grandfather's annual ritual
 On the day of his death,
During the shraddha† ceremony
 The purified water was impure;
Neither fish nor weeds could survive
 In it, and the ritual rice
And curry offered us carried
 Hospital smells of chlorine;
If the five elements conspire,
 what should we do? Tell me.

Ceremony of Loss

A tonsured head
underneath the lamplight
shining burnished copper
at mother's death
grows back the hair
in three weeks
like fresh grass
on a shaved lawn.

Bodiless, You

O Kama,[†]
Ever present
Lord of coarse tongue,

You: a presence without end
Made incarnate in all flesh
Ever in the raw,

Ever restless, never ending,
Lord god without beginning;
Lord god without end, you are

What is in between,
Not what is above on the branches,
Like the mating cranes—

As when Valmiki,[†] cursing the hunter
For taking the life of the crane,
Composed his opening sloka.[†]

You are not up there on the branches.
You are not the past or the future.
You are the visceral present,

Ever continuous, in the lightning
Act of love, reviving the moribund.
O you: archer of backbones,

Of Shunasepa's[†] strung bow,
Twister of bodies, one
Leg over a circus ball;

You, incarnate force;
You, the body electric—
The dark tip, the lingam.[†]

Lord god of both front and back,
Lord god of contraries, and
The incorporeal lingam.

Wavering Image

A piston of cigarette
inside the blue muslin
smoke around a face
is like the shaft
of sun seen through
a haze inside a room.

Two Eggs

One

When that I was a little tiny boy,[†]
I mamocked[†] the things most admired:
Butterflies in the sun, flies on jaggery,
Ants on sugar. I would lay them down
Legs spreadeagled, wings spread
Out, and I would whip their tiny legs
My head bent at my task, and
I grew up to be a master of biology.

Two

My brother aged three, gazing out of a window,
Saw airplanes in the Mysore sky.
His dreams of flying took him to war and
In the midst of battle, he remembered me
Down on the beaten earth of Mysore:
Reading a newspaper, eating two eggs
Each morning. Thinking of me
Fuelled his anger; he dropped two more
Bombs, razing two mohullas in Amritsar.[†]

Inchworm Story, Heard in America

One day
A sparrow looked around and spied an inchworm
    With inch-long fresh green body and ruby-red nose
    Arching up, inching forward, nosing along
    Inch by inch by inch by inch by inch by inch
Egoless anonymous
    Watching the worm, the sparrow grew hungry
    He caught her helpless in his beak, ready
    To swallow his catch; he heard a voice
Begging:
        Oh, oh, Mr Sparrow
        Please do not eat me.

        Obediently obsequiously,
        I measure the world.

        And the sparrow said
        Then, come to me

        My pretty worm, measure
        My tail. The inchworm made

        Haste to reply, I will measure
        Your tail dear Sir Sparrow.

        Obediently obsequiously,
        A one, a two, a three,

        A four, and a five.
        Sir, your tail is five inches long.

The sparrow thought happily, I'd hardly
Ever supposed that my tail was five inches
Long, and not a one, not a two, not a three
And thank the Lord, not a four, but a five.
Pleased with himself, he lifted the worm on
His back and away he flew to a parlia-
Ment of birds, and there they found
Many a thing to measure and compare.

Obediently obsequiously,
The inchworm measured a swan's long neck
And measured a Japanese white duck's nose
And the lifted leg of an American crane,
When an orange-coloured bird said,
Now measure my tongue.
    The inchworm trembled
    And cursed under her breath,
    Thinking, May your tongue
    Be ever so full of worms.
Cagily she measured the orange
Bird, from pink gullet to the red tip
Of the tongue, seemingly obedient,
Then on to the neck of a pelican,
The quill of a peacock, a woody
Woodpecker's red comb, the aged
Owl's bald chest and feathers of exotic
Birds known only to ornithologists.
She measured their breasts, heads,
Even entering their shameless shameful
Parts, not visible to the eye, adding and
Subtracting, computations and permutations
Till she became ungendered, a eunuch.

One day
A koel appeared, saying, measure my song.
The inchworm trembled saying, I'll do
Your tail, Sir; your beak, your mouth, your legs,
Whatever you wish; anything visible to me
I'll measure, obediently obsequiously.
But song? Who can measure your song?

The feathers of the koel bristled; he said,
        I'll swallow your inch-long
        Body, and ruby-red nose.
He was all eager to gobble her up
But the inchworm said,
        Don't, Sir, don't
        Please, do sing.
        I'll measure your song.
The koel cleared his throat and raising his
Voice, he sent his song soaring to the sky
And then inch by inch by inch by inch
Arching up, inching forward, nosing along
Pressing her ruby-red nose, now here, now
There, in circles, in gyres, slipping in, slipping out
Balancing uphill and down-dale, in shade
In sun, the inchworm measured; and before
The song was done she was gone for ever.
Anonymously silently invisibly,
She vanished for good;
No one could find her.

Unquestionably

in her dainty speech
in her sister's ready womb
in his sheepish eyes
in the pox on the middle finger
    of a man on the train
in sparkles seen during a dizzy spell
    when peering down fourteen feet deep
in the underworld's verandah
    and shattered cement floor
in the granite of sloping wall
    reflecting man and woman
the one clear certainty is the hard
    solidity of a chair.

At Night

bangles jingle
fingers play
over nose, eyes
whorl of ear
a bristle, a mustache
sprouting since morning
over December's
chapped lips,
a strand of hair
over a mole
and then
find it
again.

Upon Waking

I am nicked by a shard of glass in my singlet,
    stung by a broken bangle in my briefs,
    caught by the buckle on a rainbow-
    coloured wristband and, on hearing my son
cry in the afternoon, I gather up
the green, yellow, red slivers, to fashion for him
a kaleidoscope to view through his tears.

Yes, Yes Sir

The food you eat
    is an offering to god;
The air you breathe in and out
    is the musical scales of your mantra;
Your steps from house to street and back
    are circumambulations in the temple;
Your inebriation and rest
    are obeisances to god.

Yes, Sir, yes
    Your changing into a demon,
Changing man to woman,
    Woman to man,
Changing to the four-legged beast
    With two backs, and then
To the yoga of divine possession.

Eliminating your body's waste
    is an offering;
Spilling water
    is a libation;
Waking
    is a rebirth,
And the limbo in between
    is an intermission
Between this life and the next.

The Garland of Seasons by Kalidasa, Ritusamhara[†] in Haikus

One

Among hundreds of Sanskrit
Couplets, three fresh mango leaves.

Two

A rag doll on a hot tiled roof,
Drenching in Bombay's first shower.

Three

Coming home in a rage, he sees
The sampige[†] tree outside in bloom.

Four

Jailed for intoxication,
Or for killing a wife,
Or cursing a diplomat,

He woke in the fall, in America.
A friend sent him apples, with curving
Inch-long stems shaped like beaks.

Ravenous, he wanted to eat
Everything in sight and more.
Red apples gleamed in his eyes.

He saw polished red-hot apples
In his palm against the glitter
Of cold ruby-red apples;.

Apples weighed heavy on his palm:
From the tree, from the world outside,
And fall entered his foreign prison.

Five

After war, peace.
In the eyes of soldiers
After rain:
Summer, rain, grass.

Six

Six mallards crossing the street
Are six shadows against the mud.

Mallards on the grass, their shadows
On the grass, are without iridescence.

White birds cast black shadows,
Bird and shadow running together.

Wings flutter as the birds skim over
Water, one head with six bodies.

See white shadows of white birds on
Water, and a head with a yellow beak.

After a Sudden Downpour

at the marketplace in Rome,
    glass begins to fog;
        a haze screens this pair;
devil and doxy are
    overcome by silence, they stop
        their squabbles over shadows;
in the drenched market,
    spinning in place
        wheels turn and swivel,
school children, momentarily
    lick their chops,
            laughing at smut;

she, gazing into
    the mirror,
        adjusts with sari's edge
the kumkum on her brow;
    she checks her nose,
        eyes, parted hair;

against a faceless crowd;
    he presses his mouth
        on her opening lips;
the shop's long mirror turns
    foggy with their breath,
        erasing reflections;

he smiles shyly: he sees
    them both, buck naked

in the milling marketplace,
suit-boot and sari-blouse
        lifting like clouds after rain
        and then the sudden sunlight
breaking a phalanx of silence
        comes to, with a quickening,
                a scurrying and scattering,
plashing water from cars, buses, trams,
        after the sudden downpour
                past Italian voices.

On History

1

Mohammad of Ghor[†]
Broke Lord Somanatha's nose;
He planted seed in northern women,

And out of him sprang the Kutb Minar,[†]
A spoken language, Urdu;[†]
A musical Raga, the Megha Malhar.[†]

He left a taste for moghlai masala.[†]
And you can still see those heads he beheaded,
In the Punjab Mail,[†] and the torsos elsewhere.

2

When Grandfather's younger
Brother had grand mal-seizures
Everywhere: in the bathroom,
In the street, outside the mohullah,
We calmed his jerking limbs and clenching jaws
By inserting an iron key into his mouth;
We saved his tongue from being bitten off.

In our house of many children,
An iron key is our best legacy.

A. K. RAMANUJAN

To Hayavadana
Our Lord with the Body of a Horse

Each day,
Saint Vadiraja balanced for you a thali[†]
Of chickpeas on his head, and
Each day,
Lord Hayavadana,[†] you came to him
From behind his back, and
Each day,
You marked his arms, his face, his chest
With the imprint of your hooves, and
Each day,
He sensed your presence not only from
Your hoofs, but from the chickpea
Gas, as you broke wind.

The Body Electric

Father, Mother, the woman,
    Her nine orifices;
Her daughter named after
    A constellation of rain stars,

Krittika[†]
    Of the family tree, and when none
Of these belong to him, there remains
    His own visible-invisible body's
Eloquence: taking in or giving out,
    Speaking or dancing.

Three Dreams in One Night

Father beat him; I killed my son.
The kiss Mother gave Father, in passing,
Was given away in a dream
To the sampige-house girl;† what
Remained, went to my daughter.

> *Waking up three sleeping wives*
> *The African hero marked each one*
> *With a red hot branding iron.*

On waking, Father saw that the boy
Eliminating his body's waste
In the alley, was fondling himself,
And he right away postponed my wedding.

Passing Bells

The grandchild next door
Calls out to the grandfather.
Sitting in the autumn sun
On the lawn, he is adding the fee
For the cremation ground,
On his ledger. A cold autumn wind
Makes his calculations easier.

The rooster's cocorico at dawn,
Heralding morning's imperious warmth,
Opens the floodgates of the sun.
Light streams like rain, blue and green.
Light runnels downhill, to the melody
Of the flower raga; opaque like frosted glass—
And the telephone rings.
The baby chicks around his feet
Quill their feathers, pecking pearls of rice
From among scattered crumbs.
The telephone keeps ringing
And his granddaughter is not there to answer,
And each hour, on the hour,
It rings in front of this god,
Unmindful of the hour.
And the green of hill and the blue of sky.

And the white face of the flower raga
Turns into the white face of frosted glass
Even as the telephone rings off its hook:
Are they callers from the days
When he ran around knickerless in the yard,
Or just misdiallers of wrong numbers,

Or the slow deaf or the greedy or distant kin,
People he scarcely knows or likes,
Tongue waggers and troublers, and
A carillon of twilight bells: bells of cattle
Returning home, tinny bells of performing bears
And as someone says, bells of wedding feasts…

But the old man sits chasing in his head
Thoughts of food, fear, sex, the day's Chinese
Incident on the border,[†] his doctor's thoughts
About the Himalayas; all chasing sleep
As he sits there in the yard, he slowly
Turns into a sunbronzed garden statue.

His granddaughter comes home and finding
His arm snake cold, she screams
Her shock for all to hear. He does not wake
To say to her, hush my silly. Others close
His unseeing eyes, here at this very spot;
Here, where you and I are sitting.

•

He Had to Pay a Fine
(After B. M. Shree)[†]

He too had desired
to dress Indian verse
in English gowns
and English verse
in Indian sari

but each side tore
the borrowed togs
off the other's back
it then came to him
to dress the men in saris

and the women in pants
which drew Peeping Toms
as if at a country fair
they called him names
they thought he was lewd
they summoned the vice squad.

Translation

As when a snake moults and grows a new skin,
    When the grandson is given a grandfather's name,
    When the thread ceremony is performed,
    When there is a wedding, or the birth
    Of a son or daughter, or when there is typhoid,

Some people quote the Gita† and say, what is so
    Special? It is like: going from room to room
    Like changing saris on waking, as when
    Ovum changes from worm to sleepy caterpillar
    To waking butterfly, rebirth is the same as in biology;

Some people say, in China
    With patience the mulberry leaf becomes silk,
    But when our kitten is run over by a car, and the innards
    Are splashed and the tail is covered with gore, and
    When only the head remains intact, I follow her cry
    From room to room to the back bathroom;

My wife, feeling sad, takes a shower, and then she
    Goes outdoors to show our son and our daughter
    A butterfly fluttering its yellow wings in the sun.
    It does not feel much like a rebirth, and
    We cannot recall the right text
    About transmigration, in the Gita.

From the Table of Memory

Nothing is erased
   Even if written on
      A slate and erased;

My Goddess of Letters, Laxmi,
   My goddess of good fortune,
      Appears at the door, in Mexico.

Her finger is caught
   In the door; I ask her
      To come inside

I with my English, she with her Spanish.
   I dress her wound
      With a Kannada bandage.

The girl who used to live
   In the sampige-tree house
      Is dead: I see her almond

Mouth on the face of a prostitute
   In Hong Kong. I tell you
   Sir, nothing is ever erased.

Film Noir

Remarkably,
A newborn has eyes the colour of the sky
At dusk. In the fall, Karthika[†] is a string
Of lights in the sky, and wounds are the colour
Of betel juice in the mouths of ogres,

And green glass bangles against
The yellow of turmeric-stained hands
Of married women, and the dark green
Paste of Neem leaves[†] applied to the nipples
Of nursing mothers weaning babies,

And the whiteness of consecrated rice
And the ticklish whisper under the sheets
On a rainy afternoon, and the group
Of parrots seen framed in the mirror

As in a wedding photograph, and
The fresh green shoots on the barren branches
Of summer, looking like decorations,
And the old seed in the yellow stalk

Exploding the womb of a scorpion—all
Are to the colour-blind a film in black and white.

Disseminating Birds and a Dream

Birds in formation
　　Fly southward
　From the cold.
Geese rain guano
　　From the sky
　　　The forests thrive
　　Below their
　Flight's path.
In a dream
　I entered
　　A dark wood
　　　Where I too
　　　　Lost my way.
　　　Disseminating birds
　　Fertilize the land.
　Dark foliage
Shuts out the sky.
　I stumble
　　Out of a dream
　　　Of paper tigers
　　Devouring real sheep
　　　And see a carcass
　Lying next to
The bicycle wheel
Of the boy from
　The neighbour's house.

For A Song He Heard

Once there was a king of Mongolia;
He went on a campaign to a faraway land.
There he heard the song of a bird
That he never had heard before.
He wanted the song, so he had to catch
The bird, and along with the bird came
The nest, and along with it, the twigs
And branches, and with these came
The tree, and with the roots came
The earth under the tree and with it
The south-easterly monsoon, and so
He had to take the whole country.

He found that the whole kingdom
Had to be carted away; and so he
Assembled his elephants and horses,
The chariots and the army to fetch the bird,
The nest, the tree, the roots, the monsoon
And the kingdom, so he could never
Return to his own home in Mongolia.

Detective Story

like a police wolfhound
on the trail of a convict,

like an old friend ferreting
my location from strangers,

from mohulla to street,
from street to house,

in constant pursuit,
you invade me, you nail me.

Day's Night, Night's Day[†]

In ancient China, a clever
man, a Buddhivanta,[†] dreamt each night
    he was an orange
butterfly;

    half fluttering, half flying.
His night slid into day,
    from waking to dreaming
his day into flying night.

    Is he night's butterfly
dreaming he is a man
    or is he day's man dreaming
he is night's butterfly?

    Meta-
morphosed,
    diurnally,
he lost his mind.

Not Unlike Dushyanta[†]

at forty i wept
seeing the wooden chair and table

a physician's needle on my rear end
lost me three days

upon waking
like the amnesiac in a play

i lost the ring and forgot the reason
[why i wept].

PART 2

And Other Poems

by

A. K. RAMANUJAN

CONTENTS

Angle of Vision

He bends down to tie his laces.
Gazing up he sees twigs
Laden with white flowers.

Among the twigs with white
Flowers, one twig has two green
Leaves. He moves to take a closer

Look, and as he does, he falls into
The municipal gutter. In the arc
Of that fall, he sees the two

Green leaves on the one twig are
Changing their shape and colour
To become white flowers.

Black into White

Someone said the other day:
rare white whales are black at birth.

Bleached by salt and sun, their black
colour dissolves into sunless depths.

As their livers fatten and they grow,
water gushes into the air, from Brahma's

blowhole on their brow, and each
month, by slow degrees, they turn white.

Leviathans devour fish, give birth;
they suckle young, like you and me.

Though unlike us, they can drink
briny water from the seven seas.

They buoy up every now and then
in swirls of spume to ride the wind,

a shimmering show that dazzled Melville
inspiring his darkly buoyant epic tale.

White sperm whale and cow have
sight, no sense of smell, and their bodies

are all ears. In the seven seas, their numbers
can be counted on one hand. In the right season

whale and cow meet by chance, and should
they miss each other's Pacific mating calls

they will meet again, a few years later,
in the Atlantic or off Africa's shore.

Their gestation is elephantine; they give birth
to black-hued baby whales, two feet long.

When asleep, it's very like the Jambu Dwipa,[†]
the island where the monkey, Jambavanta[†] lived.

The gambols of a baby whale can wreck a boat at sea
and when beached: their stench can overpower a town.

The whale hunter's gold are: whale oil, blubber,
whale meat; precious as sandalwood to this day

at Parisian markets. At the time of the great flood,
Manu, the Indian Adam, and Noah of the Ark

both, found a friend in whales. Vishnu[†] in his fish
incarnation became: amphibian, man, and god in one.

Wrestlers

At sunset, having
Grappled all day
In the red mud
And having lost
The match, a wrestler
Might bury himself
Up to his neck:
A poet too.

Palace Cat

A palace with no king
Nestles in the valley
Between two blue hills.

Lagoons surround the hills
In the Italian
Landscape on the wall:

As if it were a shining
Scabbard or polished rare
Bronze coin. History, learned

By rote, is being recited
By attendants, who speak
Two different tongues.

In each room
Of the museum
Sunlight filters

Through the stained
Glass windows,
And the central dome

Displays king, queen
Horse, royal entourage;
Christ, Magdalen, and

A blue-nosed round-eyed
Straw-coloured donkey
Which Christ rides,

And under the dome
Changing colour each hour
Notice: the red carpet

Three hundred years old
And on it, a black and
White, lonely hulk of a cat.

Tukaram, Tukaram

Her house had locks:
I searched my nine pockets
For the key she gave me.
Not finding it, I became
Enraged: I slammed the door,
Kicked it, used my knees,
Shoulder, back, and like an
Elephant under the influence
I battered head-on.
Drained, and defeated,
Rage spent, I came home,
Made a cup of coffee
And drank it, intoning:
Tukaram, Tukaram,[†]
And I took a warm bath.

At Night

Asleep in his bedroll on
the threshing floor, he
dreams

he is inside a monkey. Shaking
himself awake, he climbs
down.

On the ground, the leaves
are playing cards, and he
hears

The clover trump's silent
complaint in the moonlit
night.

He reads the ledgers of moneylenders
in Banavasi[†] and the current
news

of past events in *Prajavani*,[†]
Kannada Prabha,[†] and other
papers.

From a distant future yet to be
he sees twelve constellations
smile

smugly, billowing saw-toothed
tobacco smoke from a once
wild

plant that becomes *A Poison Tree*[†]
and *Leaves of Grass*[†] and, he
reads

ancient palmleaf manuscripts
cataloguing the noise of
birds.

She

She, having forgotten
the lamentations of the trunk
in the Koka Shastra,[†]
bristles when kissed
and showers flowers when kicked.

On Objects

In a dream
    A thief with dishevelled hair
        In a yellow shirt
            Ran off from the police

He sprinted through traffic:
    Cars, bicycles, marketplace crowds
        And a procession with a band,
            When a man in a white

Shirt stood under
    The street lamp
        And stuck his arm out
            For a handshake.

The thief cried out, 'Let me go. You!'
    He ran into the alley
        Next to a warehouse
            When a man in a blue-

Striped tee-shirt and toothbrush mustache
    Seeing all this, while waiting for
        A bus, broke out
            Into a sweat.

The next day,
    At the same market
        I remembered how
            I had bought two shirts

One white, one yellow
And I asked myself,
'Did I, or did I not?'
I checked at home:

Both shirts were in my closet;
Both were dirty but smelled new.
The yellow one was tight
Around the shoulders

And had Chicago soot
Around the collar.
And underneath them
I found the striped tee-shirt.

Heard at a School for the Handicapped

'Ei-ei-ei eyes. Don't you have eyes, rascals?'
The teacher said.

'Yae-yae-yae, yes, sir,
We lye-lye-lye lied. What we have, are glass eyes,'
The student said.

'Ee-ee-ee-ears, Can't you hear? Are you deaf?'
The teacher said.

'N-n-n no, Sir. Yes-yes, we said, but we were lying.
What I have, are not ears. I wear the ear-shaped
Karna Kundala† flowers that bloom in spring.
One red, one blue. I wear them as ears at the festival of Spring,'
The student said.

'Yu-yu-yu, your head!'
The teacher said.

'We've been looking
For our heads,'
The student said,
'All over town.'

Captain Singh's Japanese Dog

Growling at night's dark face, grinning, teeth
Exposed, even sticking a parched tongue out,
Ungendered, in the heat of summer
Which blew as from a furnace in hell,
Remembering his dog kennel, he scratched
His paws on the garden gate. Snarling, he
Bit Tiger, the neighbour's dog, and at dawn
Finding the gate still locked, growled in pain
Sounding like a cock whose throat was being
Cut. Had he eaten a throwaway
Savoury, laced with poison meant for strays,
From the garbage heap? He was found
On the municipal lorry, covered in ash,
His tongue held out, eyes rolling up; he
Died, unaware of the Japanese mien
Of his origin. His mother was brought
Across the Bay of Bengal in a ship's
Hold, and had never known Japanese
Luxury; she died without so much as
A 'Sayonara'. He, a black dog,
Was given by Captain Singh's servant
To our kitchen maid. He might have lived
To old age, had someone spent eight annas†
For a dog tag. Robbed of finding a mate,
Cheated of quarrels, the groan of love's
Pleasure, of being stuck together
Copulating, straining to pull apart
From love's grip, to the glee of the street
Urchins who throw stones taunting, 'When
Will the love-drunk bitch let him go?'

The mute dog, a poor orphan, pawing at
The gate, in the moonlight, on the day
Of the festival when married women
Pray for husbands and girls beg heaven
For a suitable boy. What remains are
Scratch-mark thumbprints on a gate in need
Of another coat of paint. For dogs too
It is not enough to have a house,
Even a bloodline is required. Never forget
The dog tag around its neck with name and
Licence number. In the rubbish tips
Of municipal grounds, buried dogs are
Compost for seeds that will grow glossy
Aubergines. Beware of municipal lorries.

Gamester's Dice

The consecrated royal horse
allowed to wander where he would,
for the year,

and his attendant band of warriors, who
annex or battle for the king, lands where
the horse has been,

who honour victory with Vedic sacrifice
and eating of the horse, leaving behind
a trail of dung:

politics in England, or Chicago's patronage
are like the gamester's dice that starts the war
in the Mahabharata[†]

in which an uncle plays with dice made
of the bones of buried brothers, to claim
a kingdom.

A Nature-Culture Poem

A furry thing between the cracks,
Becomes in time, a millipede,
Then turns into a quadruped
Standing on its hind legs, but

Earth is now a nation state;
Trees are part of Forestry;
Colour's no longer colour:
Widows wear just white, but

A defeated party has colour:
Brown, or Black, or Saffron;
An elephant's teeth are ivory; ash
Is sacred vibhuti,[†] but

Brown ash signifies corruption;
Vulture fond of dove's fresh flesh
Was given righteous King
Shibi's[†] spice-fed body, and

A cow is now a party's
Emblem, in the place of
Childhood's quiet ruminant
That harmed no one.

Another on Poems

In the excitement of being born and bred
(no different from babies)
poems are all hands and mouth
and have a way of dirtying their diapers.

A Kind of Love

In a white hospital room
On a white bed, a nurse
In white, stuck a needle into
Her black unsuspecting buttocks
Counting backwards from five
Down to zero, and blast off.

Afterwards, wherever he went,
A voice within him cried out,
'Me too, me too, me too!'
In a haze, at the hour of noon
Under the melting heat
 Of the sun, he too etherized.

Dis-Ease

Seeing the cosmos in bloom
In our dooryard, he stammered:
'Hoo-who needs this?
N-n-not-ja-ja-jasmine,
No-not ro-ro-ro-roses either!'

Our teacher trashed our plants,
Tended by loving hands.
He could not breathe, he said;
The smell of cosmos
Had blocked his nostrils.

He tried a full-body massage,
He tried the neti pot[†] cure
For flushing his nostrils,
All to no avail.
The aroma of sandalwood paste,

Or the heady smell of jasmine,
Or of the yellow sampige flowers;[†]
Or the intoxicating smell of musk
From his wife's body at night,
All passed him by, he said.

A Million Points of Light

Through the single eye of an amoeba,
Rembrandt's use of shadow and light
Or pigments of the serene painting,
Bodhisattva Avalokitesvara,[†]
Would retranslate back
Into many million points of light.

Paramahansa[†] Said

A worshipper of Devi,[†]
And another man, went into a forest
For a ritual under a tree

With: yellow turmeric rice,[†]
Vermilion[†] kumkum rice,[†] raw and cooked;
Copper coin, neem leaf,[†]

And a lemon. Chanting
A mantra, he offered black puja,[†]
Invoking Durga.[†]

The scent of their offering
Came to a sixteen-foot female tiger
Who pounced on them.

She clawed and tore
The voodoo man. His companion
Ran up a tree,

But terror made him
Incontinent, whereupon the tiger turned
Away in disgust.

The man in the tree
Came to, and he saw that his companion
Was now a heap of gore

With a coil of guts
On top. He heard the buzz of flies, over
His own and the tiger's

Effluvia; he saw the colours
Of the ritual rice, the copper coin,
Neem leaf, lemon

And the grisly remains
Of his friend. He sat down in the Lotus
Position.† It was then

That the goddess granted
Him eighteen boons. He said, to himself:
'Such summons

Are not just
The work of the Devi
Alone.'

Satyam Shivam Sundaram[†]

Looking for grains
among the droppings,
a fluffy new-hatched
chick found,
Satyam Shivam Sundaram
meaning
Beauty is truth, beauty is god.

A Standing Meditation

a spinning top
motionless and still
spinning on one leg
at top speed like
a crane at rest
awake now
and then
likely to
topple
if
t
o
u
c
h
e
d
.

The Two Wristwatches

Mother died three months ago
Somewhere in Bangalore.[†]

All through the night I felt the ticking
Of the two wristwatches she had sent

The children, which arrived just a week ago.
The glow of the radium dials cut faintly

Through the night. Hugging close my son
And daughter, I could hear their pulse keep time

To the wristwatches. They will continue to keep
Time, if I remember to wind them every morning.

America, Our Common Future

From a cocoon of air
   in the birth canal
      of a fish, I swam to the shore.

      I painted a hundred times
         signs (namums[†] worn
            by twice-born men)[†]

      on the moving waters of rivers:
         the Yangtze, the Volga, the Yamuna[†]
         and the sacred Ganga[†]

         (full of the effluvia of cows),
            all flowing waters, they say;
               but cousins from lands ravaged

    by border patrols
   and those who cross over,
appear before the Supreme Court.

   All is flux—like flowing waters,
      or, as from pavilions in Mahabharata,[†]
         unmindful of the mollusk blasted off,

         the conch shell becomes
         a musical instrument[†]
            for trumpeters on Rama's Feast Day.[†]

         America! The world is as vulnerable
      as a gazelle, plagued by tornadoes,
floods, and conflagrations

We read in you
our common future; we pray
each morning for renewal,

for a new beginning.
By evening, we face disaster:
terror of bombs

terror of crime, and
next day we dream
your dreams of Utopia.

Have I Not Said†

Have I not said: if
you are born in Talkadu†
your mind will
continue to drown

in jungle waterholes.
In snowy Switzerland
don't dream of dosas;†

at wedding receptions
in America,
do not expect
pan† or kumkum.†

On Music

When the Shepherd, his teeth rotting
His blanket smelly, breath befouled
By tobacco, places a reed pipe with six
Holes on his lips;

When the Shepherd plays
His sweet music on his pipe, we forget
The rotting teeth and blanket: he is Krishna–Radha[†]
Among the sheep.

Poems by Ho Chi Minh, Composed while Incarcerated in China

1
'Even here, in jail, my sleep
Brings an eight-legged animal
Racing to touch heaven,
And I wake up.'

2
 In jail, the management
Of water goes like this:
Half a basin of water
For tea and for toilet.
If you take a bath,
You skip the tea;
If you make tea,
You skip the bath.

3
Those who looted banks
 Are given feasts; others like us
Taste the salt of tears
On parched lips.

4
All day I walk on stone
All night I feel the cold;
Even the bed bugs
Are deprived, and yet
The morning brings
Sunshine and birdsong.

5

This new jail
Smells of fresh cement
And mortar, and around it, there
Are no forests of cardamom.
I see the mountains above;
 I hear the water flowing
Underground; to the left,
Looms a giant banyan tree
That makes the day dark
And at night, it drips wet.

6

Where is freedom?
Where is liberty, protest, and solidarity?
Where? I said.

7

Constables pointed to the jail,
Superintendent's bougainvilleas
And the vermilion fencing around his house.

8

In this vast foreign jail, no leg irons are used;
there is no sound of the clanking of chains
day or night, and yet for years I have practised
carrying irons, even when walking up and down
the jail yard, my expression serious, as if
I was a supreme court judge in a procession.

Tribute to Ho Chi Minh
To Nguyen That Thanh,[†] Ho Chi Minh

O, Ho Chi Minh
Your eyes are slits.
Eleven silver threads, your beard.
Your body's wounds, stitched and unstitched
Resemble a relief map; your secret horoscope
Has become human history.
You, with your many-layered life—
You, a solitary haystack: a communist!
Your bombarded bamboo forests on fire
You found an underground
Escape route for your children.
You are a big man, Ho Chi Minh,
And yet, you are a poet,
And although a poet
You are still my friend.

Main Attraction: Bald-Headed Eagle in the Museum

A hundred thousand
   Lights were shattered
      At the Maharaja's palace.[†]
An eagle mounted
   On the museum wall
      Remains on display—

The beak, razor-sharp;
   The skull, with holes
      For eyes, gouged and
Eaten by a vulture.
   But of this event
      History remains silent
The feathers of the bald-
   Headed eagle still have
      the wingspan of a man,
Its white belly was
   Stuffed with sawdust
      For the palace museum.
Now, the wind
   Makes the wings
      Of the dead bird
Flap the air
   As in life, throwing
      Giant shadows.

Pot of Tea as Enticement

She was busy with the bath oil
Soap, towel, hammam, the clatter
Of bathing, in the purification
After menses, while I
In the kitchen, next to the bathroom,
Lit the stove and made her a pot of tea
Adding to the brew a leaf of cinnamon,
A head of cardamom and offered it to her—

Amidst that plump body's twelve scents
The soap, the incense—wanting that sensuous
Body's aroma to come close to me—
To find my body and lose myself.

A Reminder

the seeing
of the sighted
is blind, sir

you need
dame fortune.

Grandfather

In spite of the thirty-two grandchildren
He longs for his mother's breast, and is still
Taken with the colour of his own stools.
He dreams of candy in his sleep at night
And wakes to hives around his waistband.
His hand is in his own knickers and he says,
Love, love, and when the street light goes out
He sees a ghost wearing a coat; and although
His mother and father have been dead
Some years, their faraway faces come close,
Nose-to-nose with him, as he climbs the stairs,
And even when he is in court among files
Or paying fees. Blood still pumps through his
Diabetic body; he has energy
Even when inebriated; if one speaks of gold,
He displays his silver amulet in front
Of the mirror, and his eyes widen with pleasure
At the sound of bangles,[†] or the rattle in a crib.

Over a Century

Out of the grave   in the gutted town
home to the worm   and the snake, where
birds flew around   and stones lay frozen
       under the ground.

Does the tree know   it sprang from
death's compost,   or of the children
drowned that night,   or of the bomb
       or murder and prison?

Did it know   of the messages
sent from every   direction, and people
tossed about   by windstorms
       far and wide?

And was it then   you, my son, and
you, my daughter   having skipped
some generations,   came all the way
       to be with me?

A Question

Ayyo![†]
When teaching new lessons:
In grandfather's time
Gurus made the children
Stand on their heads,[†]
Sit in monkey position,
In a cloud of fumes
From roasting chilli peppers.

Ayyo!
In the Golden Age[†]
If she prayed to Laxmi,[†]
Goddess of Good Fortune,
If the barren woman would sing
And dance, wearing a medallion
Over her Mount of Venus,
Her prayer would be answered.

Ayyo!
In our times,
At a Kerala[†] festival
Of American films, you watch
A whole family of Harijans,[†]
Burned at the stake; trussed up
With thorny canes of bamboo,
And set alight. Question: for what
Reason? Answer: for drawing
Water from a Brahmin's well.[†]

Ayyo!
Like Nazis making
Lampshades[†] from the skin
Of those they gassed
In ethnic cleansing,
Did the daughter of the house
Make a new lampshade
From the skin of victims?
Would light from such a lamp
Be of a different kind?

Watch Him Fly

Watch a bird
gliding on
wings outstretched;
watch a helium elephant
on his elephant throne;
watch the guru
at Moon-Cloud junction,
on a sky-blue map
of milling streets;
see the egg-shaped bombs,
see mushrooming parachutes.
Hear the voice of the sky
body-less, out of tune
in three thousand languages
on different wavelengths,
and any new sound, now
being coined as words
by the Dictionary Committee.

In Mysore, You Speak It[†]

In Mysore
You speak it
In America
You write it
As verse
There may be
Pure cream
In a man's home
But he is not
Tempted
Some men are
Like that
When they find
Their one-eyed-one
Slumbers and
Will not rise
For wedded wife
Dejected he may
Enter his name in
Chitragupta's[†]
Register of death
To change from
Slithering snake
To walking
Elephant
To crawling turtle
Flat and frigid
He asks, O Kama
Is apathy
My karma?

A thousand
Miles from home
In a Kabuli
Madam's† den
Among wiggling
Veiled belly dancers
Memory of his
Bedded wife becomes
His aphrodisiac.

In Transit

He let his hair grow
    He smoked joints
        He went in search of outposts
            Around Kathmandu,† Alaska, Rio

In Hunsur,† he smoked
    Indian Ganesha Bidis†
        His mind swirling around
            Kathmandu, Alaska, Rio

It came to him
    During a dizzy spell
        This body in saffron nylon
            Colour of renunciation

Half-naked in California
    Next to a gurgling fountain
        On Lord Krishna's feast day†
            Clanging cymbals, or

In Chicago's darker noon, head shaven
    and copper coloured—he joined
        the Hare-Krishna† dancers, tripping
            to beatitude in clouds of sandalwood

Cave Paintings[†]

Near a prehistoric cave, you saw
Ancestors' bones dug
Up: rib cage

Of a hunter, sturdy thigh bones,
An antelope's empty socket,
The sleek head

Of a deer, jaw bones and rotted
Grinning teeth; antlers branching,
A cuneiform stick
And then

Upon striking a match inside the cave,
In the prehistoric cave,
You saw on the dank
Ancient walls

Line drawings, cave paintings of deer,
Buffalo racing in flight, even
The ones that had been
Struck

By hunter's arrows. You saw
Art eighteen thousand
Years old, and
Still alive.

Flying with the Wings of Bees

squirmy forms of life
in the wilderness
home to the worm
the ant, the bee
forms of life breeding
humming pulsing
sounding of octaves
in interstellar space
of molecules and atoms
the genealogy of
signature tunes is
in the axilla of trees
in the jungle's groin
in the lacery of webs
in the patterning of eggs
in the feelers suckling
on breast-less bodies
every pore a teat
like a second skin
of shaded stripes
squirming with life.

Observe the thorns springing
up when touched, pinpricks
and slimy green milk, leaving
threadlike black imprints on
skin, causing raging fevers.

Consider these bodies
of substance, lying in wait

till spring, some dying, some
living, to break free, crack
open, like a butterfly
with black polka dots
on red wings, light
as the wings of sprites
in the wink of an eye
during which duration
a king might age, very like
the mythic Yayati.[†]

O rich incumbents
of a bankrupt world
bringing new life out
of the blackest night
tunnelling like rodents
spinning out of your own
cells: a roof, walls, floors
finding salt and spice
in common clay, making
a cocoon from the wind
and light, sometimes
dressed in the pearls
of winter's frost
and you, the denizens
of wood can change a house
into sticks and dirt, open
to the sky, all the while
laying eggs, raising armies
of offspring, a queen bee, very
like the Chamundi[†] goddess
with six arms, survivors

all, who vanquish time
by your timeless returns.
Your raging fertility
never dries up.

Though performing
ceremonies of death each day
your birthrate never falls.
Like the enlightened ones
you have been spared
a vaginal birth: while
we who look down
on you, had to crawl
through the birth canal.

You are free from the curse
of politics. Your queen
is from the natural order.
Her body provides you
the glue that keeps
order in your granary.
Your randy males and
your sexless drones
crowd around the granary
inside and out. Your queen
commands armies and in times
of famine, your warrior forces
are ready to loot, or kill cousins:
to kill and be killed.
Your law appeared
before ours, before logos.

O you marvels, come
in; come inside this body
before incendiaries
burn history; come in, and
settling in, perform rites
of passage for the one
who asked these questions,
and as our poet said: 'Let us
fly with the wings of bees;'
'O sister, have you seen
the gossamer wings of moths?'[†]

Remember the African
killer bees from Brazil
brought there for study
and the clever bees escaped,
found mates, laid eggs, flew north
in search of better weather.
Flying each season,
multiplying hordes
on their way to the north
passing wedding parties,
school children, members
of women's clubs, funerals,
priests in habits;
struggling oppressed
migrant workers in coffee
plantations, regardless of who
or what they passed.

The killer bees from Brazil
stung their way north.

They even attacked the local
jail; the inmates thought
the venom of the killer bees
was a new sentence from
the tyrants who ruled, and before
they died, confessed to crimes
never committed.
From the year nineteen
fifty-six, the killer bees grew
into a mighty army of invaders,
advancing three hundred
and twenty kilometers a year.
In eight years, they will
have reached North America.
Committees were formed; meetings held:
in Paraguay, Uruguay, Mexico, America;
but when a native beehive
was found nesting beneath
a nuclear reactor, the army's chiefs
trembled, and grew ashen with fear.

Black is the Shadow
of What is Invisible

Quoting Jules Fernand Leger,[†]
My friend, a silver-blond white American
Said to me, 'Don't say, there are no white
Elephants. It's just that white is an invisible colour.
A black elephant is the shadow of a white elephant.'
As he said this, for a second, I could not see his face.

Teach me, O Lord

Why have you
Become silent, O Lord, before
We finished our conversation? Teach
Me, please, how to speak in my own
Natural voice, especially in matters
Of love, winnowing out the devious
And the conventional.

Erase, O Presence,
My habitual double-edged talk.
Please instruct me on how I could
Touch the minds of those on whose
Bodies I practise the scales. At least
For an instance, my Lord, reveal to me
What's in my heart.

Non-fiction

What the mother's grandmother said:

He went to a brothel, where a girl
called Malli[†] stood at the door. She held
on her head a clay lamp, glazed with cow-
dung. Under the lamplight, her shaven
head gleamed like a grapefruit. She told him
a story; it was exactly the same as
the story his own wife had told him.
The woman was no other than his wife,
A story with such a revelation
Is no story.

In Passing

Having been a snake
once, this time around,

he makes slippers
from snakeskin for

this life's wife. Much
like the Aswan Dam

built of cement and mortar,
his heart's reservoir

can stop Time's ever-
flowing river and horoscope.

For body's rise and fall
(unlike in a game of Snakes

and Ladders), the scales
of justice hang suspended

over the twelve houses
of the zodiac; and Rahu,[†]

the mythic demon, capable
of swallowing sun and moon,

causing eclipses becomes
again the snake-body,

a primeval bed[†] for
the universal Lord, Vishnu.

Beyond the Brushwood

From centuries past, white
dust from crematoriums
blown by wind, carries
the odour of death;

sand settles
in the pores, behind
eyelids, the whorls
of ears, the scalp,
the eyebrows, sand
grainy under the skin,
in folds of hidden parts;

branches toss in the wind
shaking a cloud of dust;
sunbeams turn into a haze;
and beyond the brushwood,

the horses of the sun
race along a mirage
like spinning tops.
Treading on fears:
the fear of eczema
from a brush with thorns
of the Mirza-plant,[†]
or Angel's Trumpet,[†]
the poisonous *Datura*;
the fear that feet
stung by white
leaf's scorpion claws

will shed a drop of blood
on the bright yellow flowers
with five petals. Black-
legged army ants mill
about in search of honey;
they climb the thorns
licking sharp needles.

Life lived for aeons:
women, leaving the imprint of
palms on walls they patted
with cow-dung on red clay,
homes encircled by children's
faeces and old men's phlegm,
and their afternoon's shade
from ganja,[†] genus *cannabis,*
exploding cures; their lives
spent buying and selling
wheels, lamps, needles.

View From Below

The sky is the foundation
For this home on the ground.
Here in this home, gods of the hearth
Are visible only through a telescope. These
Aspects are known not only to the photographer
On the hundred-and-ninth floor, but also to me here
Down on the ground, looking up, head tilted back.

I Believe

Actually, Blue Beard's one hundred women
are the one woman: when I think of this, she, this
one woman, in the one house, in the one mohulla,[†]
is also in a hundred places where I have stayed.

As the *Kama Sutra*[†] said, there is only one
beloved and if she knows the art of love
or if her body is played upon, she can
be as thirty-two bodies. Or, as Casanova[†]
might have said, he may enjoy the favours
of lakhs of women, but when searching
in the dark, and when touching or not
touching, again and again, he looks for
the great mother who offered her breasts at
all hours, and now, her son, weaned, knows
just the one woman, in this one place
inside his house, inside the mohulla.

Whether this is so or not, after generation upon
generation of wandering, or working in a stable
knee-deep in dung and urine, a man might find
that the birth of the prince in the stable affirms
his lineage, which is a form of salvation.

All Too Often When

In a hurry to relieve yourself,
If you were to search for an open
Field, you would find the field is actually
Someone else's house, and even if you
Were to fly to the moon on a mythic
Pushpaka[†] or were to go into the great
King's Museum, you would not be
Spared the sight of a porcelain toilet
On display in the king's collection.

During the War in Vietnam

In Saigon[†]

Unable to bear
   the torture of war,

A monk in yellow robes
   Given to non-violence,

Doused himself with gasoline
   And in plain sight,

As if holding for ever
   The posture of his protest,

He sat stiff, erect, and human,
   In a balloon of fire.

In the Sixties

Near the tiny temple
Of the Great Bull
Under the red flowering tree,
Grandmother, in the lean-to
Cookhouse, wearing no blouse,
And smelly, in her morning's
Ritually clean sari,

Woke up the street to the aroma
Of roasting coffee beans:
The neighbours' nostrils
Flaring with pleasure,
And the pregnant daughter
With a taste for garlic sambar[†]
Savouring its heady steam, in the muggy air.

As the sun rose, grandmother,
A hissing shadow by the stove,
Her backbone an electric eel of pain,
By day, opening the lid of the stew
Sighed, as if she too had heard:

Of the American Vatapi[†]
Who went to Vietnam, and burst
Out of the guts: into schools,
Films, TV, the neighbour's
Front window, and should his name
Be whispered, he would pop up
Saying, 'Here I come!'
Even here in this corner house

In Chicago, and even if in his head,
He has partaken of human flesh,
He has not the power to say,
'Vatapi be digested!'†

Again and again, at night,
The winter blizzard
Struck a shivering black stallion
Body in bed: steam rising from
Back—arms and legs thrashing
About—trees and shrubs
Sweating.

Somehow Somewhere

I am not here; I am there, and if I am
Not there, where am I? Month after month
The reason for my change of address
Remains obscure. Government regulations,
An order from above, a strike in Bandra,[†]
Murder in Bangladesh, the opening or
Closing of children's schools, a heat wave
Or a sudden frost; famine, obesity
From too much DDT, an influx of flies.
Somewhere some doctor said to someone,
'Get a transfer,' and here I am as
The replacement. I have no address
In hand. Please write to me. Somehow
Somewhere, your letter will arrive.

Our Cat Tiger[†]

Male and female
white and black
a litter of kittens
crack open their eyes.

Without discrimination
the cat Tiger
picked them by
the scruff of their necks.

She was moving house
and, did the monkey
on the verandah
observing her keep silent?

And, did he drop
from a high branch
while thinking of
another Ramanujan?[†]

By which time
our cat Tiger had
disappeared from view
with her entire brood.

Back on Terra Firma

Not finding
Once upon a time's
Flying carpet, seven-league
Boots, nor chariot, palanquin
Or horse, and these days
Rickshaw, taxi, airplane—
Not finding even these,
Or, the angels, winged
And swift as the mythic
Airplane Rama and Sita
Flew. There was nothing
To carry me, but a nameless
Lame man who let me ride on
His back, up the slope
Carrying me from the valley
Below. Poor man! He brought me
Back to earth, peeling off illusion.
The story might have ended there,
But the sky whitened, and
Lust and greed for power
Were unleashed; I said
'Sir!' and I took off in haste
One foot in front of the other
Left foot, right foot, left, right,
Not heeding zodiac signs
Of Pisces and Aries. I ate
Goat and fish, according to
The dharma of convenience.†
A stray dog in Shanghai
A hissing snake in Bangkok
Hopping pan-fried frogs in Paris

And in Nepal, five soothsaying birds
Defeathered the moment
They foretold the future, to be
Fried and laid out on their backs,
A repast to stuff the mouth
Imbibing liquor in ten towns,
Tasting the tangy sweat of the girl
From Nagaland,[†] missing a turn
In spite of the map or compass point,
Eyes blurry even with binoculars:
Yes, I have gone far, and now I have
To buy a new kind of boots.

PART 3

Kuntobille

by

A. K. RAMANUJAN

CONTENTS

Hopscotch

In the back lanes
　　Of our houses
　　　　　Girls play hopscotch
　　　　　　And boys as well
　　　　　　　Till the age
　　　　　　Of puberty.
　　　　　One leg up
　　　　One leg down
　　　Body stretching
Hopscotching
　　From square one
　　　To square two
　　　　And then reaching
　　　　　The last two squares
　　　　About turn
　　　　Hopping jumping
　　　To the base
Near mother's house.
　　　The same as black and white
　　　　And yellow children
　　　　　In narrow alleys
　　　　　　Far away
　　　　　In Germany
　　　　In Africa
　　　Except for those

Whose limbs were
    Wasted by bombs
       Or polio.
          I can
               Observe Africa
          In the house
        Next door.
      I can see Germany
Across the lane
      And in the dust
        To my wonder
           I now perceive
        The visvarupa[†]
      Or design and pattern
Of the universe.

Old House Revisited

1
Out of a poem
By an American
An elephant leapt out.
He broke into the house,
His head went
Through the roof
He tore down the house
With Yankee impudence.

2
Half a century ago
The baby elephant
Crossed the royal stable
And came to the house
To play with us; now
He, a black bull elephant
Has come to our front yard
For the youngest
Daughter's wedding.
He tore off the bananas
From the canopy, and I
A grandfather in his dotage
With dried up dewlapped skin
Came out, forgetting eyeglasses.
I blinked under the lights
And could make out
A large black cloud
I patted his back
And retreated, feeling sad
I could not ask him to come inside.

3

In sixty years, I grew just sixty-six inches
The old house in which I was born
Is sufficient to this day.
A colony of children, grandchildren
Brothers-in-law and sons-in-law
Reside there, scarcely visible.

4

If the black bull elephant
Were to come inside the house
The door, the roof, the ceiling, and festive
Wedding tents and even the second floor
Would have been destroyed.
Elephants, they say, have strong
Memories, but thankfully
He had no memory of me.
It was I who remembered
The elephant's story.
I gave five rupees† to
The mahut† for a bunch
Of sweet bananas; indoors
The house grew suddenly small.

Twin Birds from the Upanishads[†]

In the fork of a guava tree sat two birds:
One was pecking, picking, and eating
From hunger and thirst,
The other sat still
Watching.

And every sweat pore in his body
Became an observant eye.
Just so, next door:
Husband, wife
Family.

Haiku, Zen-1

First
This hill, that hill
This river, that river
    When body touches body
    The hill is not a hill
    The river is not a river
And again
This hill, that hill
This river, that river.

The Ekka Plant

Chewing red peppermint,
Walking from school,
We pass the Ekka Plant[†] house.
Plant of ill omen,
Plant of the Devil,
Ash-smeared bud, and tumid bloom.

When the leaf, branch, or stem is torn or cut
The Ekka oozes a gummy milk.[†]
To one side of the plant
Stood a dead man's door,
And to the other, a window.

At the door without a roof,
At the door without a threshold
Almost inside, there was another Ekka,
With a long tumid flower, and ash-smeared bud.

Now the Ekka returns to me,
Not as a trick of memory
About our distant past
When we walked home past it.
The fear of the plant
Returns to me, even now.

At the Museum

A fourteenth-century Ming dynasty antique
Bed frame stood lonely and resplendent.
Carved from teakwood, once rising, tree above tree,
On the hills of Indochina, and now extinct
To their very roots. When the groom was a crawling infant
And the bride a babe in arms, they were betrothed.
That very day, a tree was cut; chopped inch by inch,
Chiselled year after year, by the carpenter's family,
The son taking over at the death of the father
And the son-in-law after the son died of a stroke.
Their craftsman hands carved lotus flowers,
A bunch of leechi fruit, a Chinese crocodile,
The fish, the tortoise, and signs of their horoscope:

Tortoise, goat, and spreadeagled twin-headed
Dragons breathing fire. The bed took sixteen
Years to be done; the bride and groom came of age,
Studying: writing, math, cooking, fencing, knitting;
She with a pony tail and breasts, he with a mustache
And manly voice, were ready for their nuptial night.
Chinese silk draped the mattress; the bed frame stood
Ready for generations yet to be. Once the palace
Caught fire, one side of the bed turned black;
Yet, it is still on display for such as I.

A Poem by Anna Akhmatova†

I will appear in your dreams as a black ewe,
On withered, unsteady legs
I will approach you, begin to bleat, to howl:
'Padshah, have you supped daintily?
You hold the universe, like a bead,
You are cherished by Allah's radiant will...
And was he tasty, my little son?
Did he please you, please your children?'

An Enchanted Flute
(After Rainer Maria Rilke's Sonnet 1:1)[†]

The tree is growing, growing beyond control,
As cowherd Krishna[†] is playing his flute.
Hear the silence, O tree in the ear.
The new silence has sixteen signs and changes.
The worm of life is created by silence;
It is shaped by crystal from the caves
Of the forest. The silence is not from
Guile or fear. It comes from intense listening.
Grunting, barking, or roaring would sound
Like opposites to those, who were intent
On nothing else, who were listening till now;
And as dirt, sticks, or bombs at the gate, are
About to fall, O Krishna, you build, in
The caves, in the listening ear: a temple.

Deep Sea Diving

if
after finding a handful of pearls
at three hundred feet below

if
under pressure from nitrogen gases

if
from fear of the knifing saber-faced swordfish
lying in wait behind the branches of blue coral,

if
he were to surface in haste, climbing the ladder, rung by rung
the pressure released would cause such distress, as

if
opening a soda pop, the bubbles were to enter
his animal heart and he would cease to be;

if
once more, they were to send him down three hundred
feet to dissolve the bubbles, slowly, foot by foot, and

if
they were to lift him up layer by layer, blue bubbles
rising, one at a time, in reverse, to become the breath of life

how would I ever know
if
this is true or not true.

As Joachim Maria Machado says

A poet is a fisherman.
A fish caught in the ever abundant river,
Was alive but minutes ago. It came up
Struggling, wriggling, flashing
Out of reach of the fisherman.

For poets with good karma
This magic is possible,
But in the hands of those like us,
The fish we catch will die rotting
Without its last lightning flash,

And yet again, for some others
Fish is food on the plate
And a crisply fried
Dish of fish is for them
An offering from the river.

A. K. RAMANUJAN

Unlike Descriptions
(After reading Rilke's *The Book of Hours: Love Poems to God*)

Peering closely at a picture
And then stepping back a few feet,
Seeing perspective

Rewards the same way as when
A rare word suddenly reveals its meaning.
Or, it's like noticing for once

The cooking utensils you use daily;
Or, seeing Mother's face
Or, the ship that brought you

Safe home, through a storm at sea.
None of these are like descriptions
Of things as they seem.

Haiku, Zen-2

The river of life flows full
On the shore; the store
    sells the water.

Haiku-3

She frowned upon:
Body, as body,
Drama, as theatrics,
Poem, as just words, words.

All earned opprobrium.

For Some

At dusk, the words:
On the edge of the forest
The hour of blooming...
Will give goosebumps
Even if under the hot sun,
But our man
Gathering spring's pumpkin
Flowers on the cowpats
(Buzzing with bluebottle flies)
For the Pongal[†] festival,
Sees a butterfly
Fluttering five colours
While laying eggs in the ear
Of the Buddha statue, razed
By Muhammed of Ghazni.[†]

A Reel Played Over and Over

I may have told you before: it seems
But yesterday, I came from Mysore[†]
To Hyde Park. If I count correctly
Twenty-five years have passed: as if a year
Is but a day, a day but an hour, an hour
But a minute—a cipher to lidless eyes.

As I said: I may have told you before,
It feels like just yesterday I came
From Mysore to Hyde Park, or am I
Imagining the Bangalore train,
Bombay taxi, British P & O,
New York cab, Chicago bus, all one
Behind the other? I was young, green-eared,
Carrying in my suitcase, secured with a rope—
The key having broken—a single blue suit,
Ten tubes of Neem toothpaste[†] that Mother had
Packed, thinking, they won't have it there.

Then followed: marriage, work, California,
Children, moving from eight rented houses,
Carrying along back-breaking furniture;
The older one, a girl, already twenty-four,
The boy twenty-two, and yet it seems
But yesterday, I came here from Mysore.
I've already said this; please excuse me;
When you visited me here yesterday,
Did I say this? While completing this
Long sentence, yesterday is already
Tomorrow. It's like going to Outer
Mongolia on an airplane: a student

Who left there yesterday, arrived here
The day before yesterday, losing one
Whole day, and that too, mark, a Monday.
Where did the day go? And wondering about
It, she felt giddy losing herself for two days,
Like when the Hindi film calendar pages
Were whipped up noisily, with air blown
From the film-studios, and the birthdays, new model
Cars, skirts, hair colour, newspapers, presidents,
A coup d'état in every city they had
Heard of; the burning buses, the Sri
Lanka hotel where they stayed the day before,
Bombed the next day, and from every direction
Came: AIDS, cancer, an earthquake killing relatives,
Friends and enemies, and after four failed
Marriages; after gin, after being bitten
By a snake or worm in the Amazon,
One man having perished at a jungle picnic
Fire, and now picture please, the ripening
Old man and woman. Some fight old age,
Others have to surrender quietly
To time, and become water, earth, smoke
And ash, and finally the ever-present dust.

By Gary Snyder

Roof leaked for
Many weeks;
Moving just one tile
Stopped the leaking.

Same as in Childhood

As he lay dying, he
Saw between the rafters
Same as in childhood

A baby lizard
Stone-coloured
Its tail cut off,

Cheep-cheeping,
Its heart beating
Dub a dub a dub.

The River

a
rivulet
seeping through sand
past rock and cave
flowing, descending
down the mountain's face
from a trickle
to a mighty roar
along a mile-long tunnel
down
frosty
sheer mountain
to the green valley below
river whirlpooling past the dam
past the town of burning ghats†
the effluvia of the living: a river of life
washing livestock, bathing people
entering houses, washing interiors
quietens into the river of peace
providing water for rinsing
the mouth, offering
generously the last
trickle, having come
from dark caves
to a sunlit place
oh river, you
entered
me.

Drinking Gin

An ahiramruga[†]
    came to me
I have never
    seen an ahiramruga
Is ahiramruga
    in Africa?
I have never
    been to Africa
None of the zoos
    ever owned
Ahiramrugas
    I don't recall
A signpost
    displaying one
Or a photograph
    and yet, as I drank
I thought of
    an ahiramruga
Not just one
    but two
Male and female
    and from them
Grew flocks
    of baby
Ahiramrugas.

A Story Told by Menelaus[†]

Ramanujan's Kannada poem 'A Story Told by Menelaus' is the next poem in the Kannada text. On translating it into English, it turned out to be an exact close translation of Robert Fitzgerald's English translation from the Greek, of Homer's *Odyssey, Book Four, lines 317 to 439*. In this instance, Ramanujan made no changes or additions. There was nothing to be gained in translating a translation back into Fitzgerald's version. Therefore 'A Story Told by Menelaus' is not included in *Poems and A Novella*.

When in Your Mind You Are

floating in a coffin on your back,
standing colossal as a naked rock-hewn Jain statue,
eating grapefruit in segments,
devouring red meat like a carnivore rakshasa,[†]
growing thorns on nails, or face, like a rose plant,
rolling in motion, like a cart's wheel
turning into food for worms, eating and being eaten,
you fertilize plants and trees in two weeks, and
wearing a mud pack on your head, you sprout seeds on a twig,
standing firm on your feet in a Jerusalem marketplace,
or a crossing between cars in Chicago, looking for a footpath,
you wake up and you are a man once more.

Arrival In America

In room forty-one
Of an antique hotel
On fifty-second street,
I closed the bathroom door
And turned on the tap:

Water, red as blood, spurted
Gurgling from unused pipes.
I waited for a long time
For the water to turn clear;
I am still waiting.

On a Single Day

When the mercury in the thermometer
Drops, the fever in the brain rises,
When eating rice at lunchtime
Images of consuming buffalo dung
Flashes into my mind.

Same as when the wife's face
Turned into that of a fox
The daughter's face, a mongoose
And the son's, a howling hyena.
These images damage the heart

And fracture the soul.
In the afternoon I saw thousands
Of marbles of varying sizes and colours
Fashioned out of precious stones
That unknown good men, strangers,

Scattered pell-mell on the floor.
White, red, black, purple, lemon-yellow
Tangerine-yellow, turmeric-yellow
Jaundice-yellow, the terracotta colour
Of a monk's robes; dark-green, mango-green

Leaf-green, parrot-green, ash-pumpkin-green;
Colours of the spectrum: scattered around.
I picked each up and felt them, and wiped
Them clean, and separated them by colour
Forgetting laughter, grief, bile, wife,

And my children. I spent the day
At my appointed task, and by evening
I had grouped the gemstones by colour,
Perfect for meditation. I thought,
I'll make holes to string them together.

I left them as they were for another day;
Then I shook them free and let them fall
Pell-mell on the floor, as before.
After dinner with my wife and daughter—
I had not thought of them the whole long day,

I played cards and laughed to myself
Remembering the sand-coloured faces
Of the fox, the mongoose and the hyena,
And now seeing them restored to normal,
I was moved, but I did not cry.
Instead, I wore a slight smile.

1940 Perhaps

Father's elder sister and husband
Came to our Mysore home.
At night, we children were assembled
In a room upstairs for a shadow play.
Father's lamp, behind a makeshift
Bed-sheet screen, threw shadows
As fingers began to play a wondrous show
Of flickering magic shadows:
A mewing cat with ears perked up
A dog that barked and snarled and bit
A duck with beak into its feathery tail
Staring at us through a tiny hole of an eye.
Repeatedly, we saw: a finger, ten fingers
One hand, two hands, and moving images
On a white sheet: mewing cat, barking dog,
Itching duck, a comic strip of shadows.
Our visiting uncle's hands had practised for
Forty-eight years, and with him stood his wife
Father's elder sister, whom we knew as doddathe,[†]
And Appa, and Amma[†] in the upstairs room
And as I write this page, I am there, in front,
And behind the bed-sheet screen, this moment.

Reason for Not Composing Sun and Moon Poems

having swept the house clean,
brainstorming day and night for a poem
he saw the moon had failed to rise over
the river, and when it tardily showed up,
the poet found his sleep had fled, and when
next he awoke, the sun was at the window,
and he could see above the shelves, a crowd
of calendars of other years. Slowly waking
then, scratching and yawning, he saw the ash
in the hearth. Stoking the ash
the watching waiting mind of the poet
wanted a bidi;† he smoked the handrolled
cigarillo on the veranda, by which
time, the moon had left the river
and swallowed the stars; she tried
to come in through the window
but the yellow moon could
neither come in nor go out.

Feeling Guilty While Drinking Coffee

The bones inside my body were stolen
    From others while they slept.
I am a thief, a sinner: is there no end to sins?
    Were I not born, some poor man
Would have been drinking this cup of coffee.
    I tell you, I am a thief, a sinner.
Is there no end to sinning? In January's
    Cold, the body of mother earth
Is filled with dust raised by the living:
    Landfills, dead calves, discarded
Banana leaves used at dinner. I feel
    Like walking from house to house
Knocking on doors, begging someone, anyone
    For forgiveness. I want to share
With someone, anyone, the bread baked
    In the burning kiln that is me.

A Deer-Skin Rug in Colorado

In Colorado's sandy forest
Near a Deerpath Inn
When cars revved their engines,
One, two, three, four, five deer
And another with white fur
At the tip of its tail
Turned around, and gazed
Enquiringly in the direction
Of the sound of our cars.

The great antlered bucks,
Glossy cow, and baby fawn
Stopped, and stared in the direction
Of the sound. In our hotel, the same
As in old houses, a deer-rug,
Eight feet long, was on the floor.
The walls displayed antlered heads.
Outside, there was sand
And furze, and a road.

What He Did Not Know

Left with one lip
   How can he eat?

Left with one wing
   How can he fly
   From tree to tree?

Must he hop
   From the foot of one
   Tree to the next?

Even under
   Fall's mellow sun
   He feels disabled.

Suddenly Cold, I Shiver

In the bedroom: under
My feet, dead wife's tangled hair.

Inscape
Based on a Poem by Yehuda Amichai

I own: three or four changes of clothes
But in a life of changes, up or down,
My death is the one certainty.

God is far away, and I have doubts
About whether he exists at all; my elders are
Wheezing, cancer has come to a friend;

Outside town, a murderous army of children
Are crossing the border with bombs, and yet,
In spite of all this, I feel: all's well with me.

Pushing my leg into black flannel trousers,
Pulling down shirt, pulling up zipper's grinning teeth,
Buttoning shirt, tightening belt, I feel: all's well with me.

From centuries untold, from the gore and flesh and pus,
From eating tidbits at the table of the Vedantic spread,[†]
And the Planet of Love, this body born by accident,

Tossed about, kept awake by the ladle scraping
The bottom of the barrel, I found I could slip out
Of my trousers, and say, I feel: I am not bad after all.

A Meditation

In the course of a meditation
I thought all day I was a black
walnut tree.

That evening, the golden
retriever from the yellow house
sniffed me

as I stood waiting for the traffic
light, lifted its hind leg
and honoured me

with its warm piss.

In the rainstorm that night, the tree
toppled with a great crash and lay
there, its roots

were an exposition in the sky.
The municipality came
with electric

chainsaws, cut it up in convenient
pieces, loaded them in their truck
and took it all

somewhere.

The carpenter worked with his handsaw,
smothered it with sand paper, polished it
with bees' wax,

made a butcher block table and
a butcher block chair. The paper
factory ground up

the bark and the leaves into a pulp,
patted it, bleached it, and turned out rolls
of paper

with a logo in a watermark.

Now here I sit in this chair,
paper and pencil on my table,
and as I write

I know I'm writing now on my head,
now on my torso, my living
hands moving

on a dead one, a firm imagined body
working with the transience
of breathless

real bodies.

On Tenali Rama's[†] Gesture as a New Interpretation of the Ramayana.[†]

I leave letters
And letter writing alone.
If I reply, I do not mail them.
If I send them, the letter never reaches anyone.
If they reach, no one reads them through.
If my letter is read, the meaning is misread.
Need you ask?

In poems,
Even misinterpretation
Is another form of interpretation.
Even poems about the detritus of life
Are worth reading or writing or discussing.
Every verse speaks. The word is the gold
Nugget in the sand.

It's the silver nerve
In the ore. Even the nearsighted
Will spot gems. This brings to mind,
Tenali Rama, the court jester of the King
Of Vijayanagara. He was asked,
'How did Sri Lanka burn?' 'Like this,'
He said and he set fire to the house
Of the one who asked.

The Model Inside

An August wind scattered my son's papers
And threw around accounts in the office.

The glass paperweight common in these parts
Has afloat in it: a house, water, door, window,

A sloping roof, a yard, a blue tree
And snow flakes. If you shake the glass globe

Water hits the sky, snowflakes come down
On tree and house, and in two minutes,

The snow stops; everything is calm again.
In August, I hold in the palm of my hand

December's snowfall, and in December
Fresh white flakes come down endlessly

From the sky. At that time, the children,
Holding the paperweight in their hands, watch

The snow falling inside the glass globe
For two minutes at a time. Beyond

Their view: sun, rain and wind: rage and stop
Like life after death, when the outside

Is the model inside, seen in a glass,
As if from another dimension.

Bound and Flayed

This man and woman separate
And their embranglements increase:
Talons sharpen, as if caged birds,
Let loose, were to go at each other
From the claw-tracks of troubles.
He falls asleep, and he dreams:

In this dream, the birds
Avoid the poisoned rice, and
Flapping their wings, they escape.
When a hunter aims a shot
And yet another shot

He segues to a second dream.
If the poet Valmiki[†] had watched
The killing of the crane as an amusing
Sunday sport, the story of Rama and Sita
Which he composed, in response
To the killing of two birds in love
Would have been a different story.

Anthills would have cracked
Open around them; even the faithful Sabari,[†]
Tasting each fruit before offering it to Rama,
Could not have helped, and Sita's lock-up in
The forest would have needed a thousand
More eyes to express her sorrow.

But our pair: this man, this woman,
Tied, bound, flayed, untroubled by epic
Anthills, their lives conjoined, blighted,
Brimming with dreams unrealized, know
How best to tighten the knots on the noose.

Personae

One

He once ate thirty eggs
Drank litres of almond milk,
Won the marathon at the Asian Games;
Today, he hobbles on a wooden leg
And feels a dull ache in his stomach.

Two

An advertisement for Nirodh†
Decorating the wall, says,
'The son for fame
The daughter, a sacred flame.'
But in this family
The daughter won fame
The son brought shame.

Three

Typing for ten years each page
He still makes a hundred errors.
After cooking for twenty years
There is too much salt in the soup.
After writing thirteen novels
There is nothing to show
That even a goat would touch.

Of the thirteen miscarriages,
One, born on the bathroom
Floor, was one-eyed and had thin
Legs, as if from a wet dream.

Four

An Irish quadriplegic, Christie,
Paralysed from birth, types with his toes
Novels, and autobiographies. Admirers
Shower his fist of a body: confetti
Of appreciation. They shake his fingerless
Hands; they cover him with medals,
Honours, degrees, and the whole town
Carries him about, crying, hurrah,
Hurrah for Christie.

Please Note

No, it does not surprise me
That the hidden bones
Of my mildly aching body
Will burn and turn one day,
Be bleached by the sun,
Become fodder for a dog's jaw,
And I too will sport a lipless grin.

On Crying†

We, the lachrymose,
Might marvel at a bitch,
Or wonder about the dry-eyed
Cow that has lost a calf.
There's rarely a report of
A sobbing monkey. I don't hear
Of a tiger, lion, or deer in tears,
Even under lock-up in a zoo.
Tell me, do cats ever cry?

Unlike bodies of water,
Unlike baths in ancient sites,
Human tears leave no markers
As rivulets do. Tell me, didn't
The people of Mohenjo-Daro† weep
When faced with destruction?
In some countries: people cry open-
Mouthed, even in the Halls of State.
In some, they cover their face

Or go behind the bathroom door.
In some places: only children may cry;
In some others, women may let it rip.
For a man, it's different: tears are allowed
If the mother dies, or, while watching
A Tamil film in a darkened theatre; others
Will say, 'Look! He is crying like a baby.'
Then, there are others who may burst out
Laughing when they feel like crying.

An Uncommonly Common Man

Wanting a cane, he swipes a white cane
From a blind man. He has in mind St Vemana[†]
Who pawned his wife's jewellery, and nuptial
Mangalsutra,[†] to raise money to pay
A prostitute, who was twelve years old,
For a whole year's service.
In Thailand, at a conference of vegetarians,
He slips away, on his own, to a native eatery,
Where they keep under the counter, four
Prodigious snakes. He picks the one
He fancies; they dice it, with snake liver,
To make fritters. A few days of such fare,
And he is no longer hungry.
He is in Heidelberg, and with new
Friends he goes to see a belly dancer. He
Never returns home. His mother, sister,
And wife, shift from saris to dresses
To work in a shop in the garment
District, where they work day and night
To keep afloat. Just once, he called them
From Paris; he sent them a postcard
Of a Van Gogh sunflower.
Such moral turpitude is common in midlife.
Our common uncommon man does not go in
For murder or looting; he commits sins
For which there is no earthly justice.
What he gets is a slow burn in his heart,
And his story makes a hackneyed
Subject for a play.

A voice inside him will forever intone,
'Sinner, sinner, shame on you!' and once
In a while, another voice will say, 'No, let it be;
It's not you who sinned, but someone else, who
Carries your name,' giving him respite from
That other voice saying, day and night,
'Sinner, sinner, shame on you!'

On Quests

Having missed what was under
their noses, they spent years
on a quest:

Thriving friends have spent their lives searching
for the Koh-i-noor;[†] or a register of Nalanda[†]
students, at the medieval university;
or Charles Darwin's tortoise-
like Galapago Islands; or
the secret handbook
for Nazi torturers,
or the confidential
path of an AIDS virus,
or the blue whale's sperm
or the farthest cosmic nebula
then as now, or my blood's
secret genealogy.
If someone had not said,
'That's not do-able, little fellow,'
I too might have been like them.

In their quest
what was far would have
been near, coming nearer,
oceans becoming the shore,
shore the house, tree, field,
and the wind on the face,
all these were like spilled
mercury on hands or eyes,
for those accustomed
to telescopes and microscopes.

Now here, a moment later,
there, beyond touch, visible,
and then invisible,
moving to slow decay,
minute by minute,
this bodiless demon
with woman face,
keeps winking, enticing, smiling
from the mercury behind the mirror.

They may cross the Amazon,
but how cross the internal Ganga;[†]
how can they touch each day's horizon,
or the mindscapes within?

Mahavira's Story[†]

Having harpooned a whale, he escaped
and hunted a tiger.
His karmic debt was paid off when bed
bugs feasted on his blood.

House of Wood

A tornado shook the house, wrecking
The contractor's steel ladder.
Built of wood, the house
Itself withstood
The storm.

O Lord, Whether You Exist or Not

1

Whether You exist or not, O Lord.
The word, You, makes me search
For reasons, even though eons ago
All this was inscribed as my fate
And, how can I, a babbling man,
Talk to *You*, who are beyond words?

2

Those who know You best, say:
You are in the tree, the house, the bamboo
Tray carrying gifts; You are in stone,
In the sound of sheep bells, in the mill,
In the bull, in the wind; in water bubbles,
In wheezing mucus. I can continue
This list, even though you are invisible.

3

The Michigan apple tree in March
Has taken on new leaf, buds, white flowers:
Within a month, the flowers
Will have gone, and the tree will sag
With green-red apples, and below,
Under the ground will remain, the hidden
Upside-down treetop of roots.

4

If I cut the tree, I will find
Its memoir of rings, further proof
Of the theory of evolution.
Yet, a question comes up: why

Do the buds slowly, very slowly
Like a slow-motion bomb
Quietly continue over the years

5

Growing branches daily to become
Monumental, sixty feet wide,
Home to worms, birds, and life, for eighty
Years, and when drying out, each atom
Will drop to the earth, from whence

6

It sprang. They say, You are the essence,
You are the root, as when I bite
Into a radish and feel the sting.
I find no rest in faith or doubt.

7

What's left? Intimate talk? Ignorant
Though I am, sixty-three generations
Are behind me. They were far more
Intelligent than I, yet even they found
No relief from: fire or rain or flood.
They did not cry out when
Maimed or killed. In spite of,
They surrendered to You
They were Alwars,[†] drowning in you.

8

Whether drowning or floating,
They addressed You, using thousands
Of names in three thousand languages.
They called out to You, as if to a baby,

They worshipped You, as if you were a king,
They flirted with You, their lover; being
Romantic, they kissed You, kissing the air.
Men loved You, as if they were women
They menstruated, adoring you.

9
Women grew hot from loving you
They became lovesick, their guts
Twisting, they lamented your
Absence, found solace in suffering,
Went crazy, or grew weary.
They wrote poems, far better ones
Than this one, using meter and rhyme.
Their utterances were coloured by loan
Words; their dreams reached
You, to the realm beyond speech.

10
They found words to describe You
And I have borrowed words to say:
Master of Silence, whether You
Have the one face or the thousand
Faces, whether You are to be covered
With garlands of songs, and words
Of praise from the white light
Of Vedanta† from under the dark
Cupola† of the temple's silent bell.

11
Your voice is drowned by the sound
Of the ocean. And Your eyes seem
To close as soon as we open our
Practised mouths to sing Your praise.

12

You own us all, and yet You
Have sued Your devotees;
The defendants have escaped;
The court has been in recess
For centuries; my house was
Searched; my mouth is bankrupt:
It drools and smells foul.

13

My teeth ache, become loose,
And drop off one by one.
My longing for supari†
Keeps me awake at night.
My leftover words grow stale.
Toothless, I eat mud. My bones
When shaken, sound like a rattle
That could please the Infant Krishna.

14

Only the dead can get a glimpse
Of You, O Lord, who have been
Invisible. What I need is proof
Of your existence. Are you not
Present in the round earth,
In the glittering stars, in the world
Of vegetable, animal, and worms
And in millions of icons—as also
 In torture, in killing, in lovesickness,
In chaos, and even in the laughter
That spreads to the four corners.

15

You might have dug in deep
Like the branching roots.
I remember You: like the way
We think of our dead children;
Like the memory of mother's
Breast; the mother who nurses
Six or seven times a day and then
Weans the child with bitter
Neempaste applied to the nipples.[†]

16

Yet, you come to my mind like
The memory of Mother's nipples.
You are like the broken promise
Of a husband; like the ritual
Pollution from the death
Of distant kin; You come to mind
Even when I am high or drunk.

17

Even when struck by tragedy
The grammar of our native tongue
Never deserts us. You are: He
Who resides in my consciousness,
No matter what names I call You by,
But please note: our dog does not need
You, nor our apple tree in the yard and

18

The stars in the sky do not need you.
My disbelief is as real as my flesh.
You are like the embrace of a guest
In a train speeding in a foreign land.

You are: like burning desert sand,
Like the bloodied face of a Nazi friend.
Thoughts of You persist in me:
It is as all-consuming as
The jealousy of a second wife.

Marana Sarana

Not listening to the gods,
Ignoring practice,
Unmindful of precept,
He reached a drying river bed.
Marana, sarana.[†]

Imagining the demon fish to be
Hungry, in the drying river bed,
He began a fast from sheer pity,
But hunger took him by surprise.[†]
Marana, sarana.

His body's dependence on food
Began to crave for spring lamb,
For heart, liver, whole eggs, all
Smothered in spice, all taboo food.
Marana, sarana.

Insatiably, he grew as plump
As the demon fish; he entered
 The river, roiling with silver fish.
He became as one with fish and river.
Marana, sarana.

A baby fish suckled his thumb
The fish gamboled, he frolicked,
Eye to eye, mouth to mouth, winking,
Praising kin and next of kin.
Marana, sarana.

He said, 'All I have is yours.'
Being of a literal cast of mind,
The fish began to feast on him,
Eating, and being eaten.
Marana, sarana.

Brahma Jnana: A Silent Sonnet†

u—uu, u—u –u
uu u—u –uu.
—u uuu –uu
u—u uu—u uu

– – —u uuuuu,
—uu –uu—
u uuu –uu—u
uu—u. –uuu,

– –u uuu – – –
uuu –u u—u
– –u—u uu-

uuuu? –u, uuu
– – – –uuu –u
uuu —u—uu?

Notes on the Poems

(*These notes were written jointly by Shouri Daniels-Ramanujan, Krishna Raju and Prithvi Shobhi*).

NO LOTUS IN THE NAVEL

A King of Soliloquies, p. 5

Mithuna: Sexual union; *Lagna*: An auspicious hour/time. *Mithuna Lagna*: The hour of the constellation Gemini, an auspicious period for weddings. The narrator of the poem received an award from the Kannada Association on the day his beloved was getting married. Since mithuna also refers to sexual union, here the narrator, who was ditched by his love, says that instead of making love to his bride on their wedding night, he had to masturbate.

A Meditation on Doors, pp. 8–9

Dwarake: A city in western India, which was built by Lord Krishna.
Tribhanga: A standing posture in which the figure is curved at the waist and neck to form an 'S' shape.
Kama Sutra: An ancient sexual manual on erotics.

Connections, pp. 10–12

Radha-Krishna love songs: Radha is Lord Krishna's consort. Their love is considered pure, ideal, and exemplary.
Sampige: Sampige flowers (Campaka in Sanskrit), blossoms of various colours from the tree *Michelia campaka*.

Hanumanta Temple: Temple for the monkey-god Hanuman, or Hanumanta. In the prayer ritual at dusk, one uses a lighted lamp.

Maharaj Jai Singh's Jantar Mantar: An astronomical observatory housing a huge sundial and other masonry instruments built in 1724 in New Delhi by Maharaja Jai Singh II of Jaipur.

Vamana and Trivikrama: Vamana, a short dwarf, a Brahmin, one of Vishnu's incarnations begged for food at the court of the demon king, Bali. The king assured Vamana that anything he wished for would be granted. Vamana asked for three steps of earth. When the king granted the wish, Vamana grew into Trivikrama, a giant. With one step Vamana/Trivikrama covered the entire earth, with the other the skies, and he asked the king where he should put the third step. Upon realizing that Vamana was Lord Vishnu, the king bowed his head. Vamana/Trivikrama placed his foot on the king's head and pushed him into the earth.

Mandala: Circle, magical concept of circles within circles.

Rahu and Ketu: At the churning of the oceans, a demon, appeared in the guise of a god to receive the divine nectar (amrita) which gives immortality. The Sun and Moon warned Lord Vishnu, who then split the demon's body. Seeing that the demon had partaken of the divine drink and had become immortal, Vishnu let the head and tail survive in the heavens as Rahu and Ketu. They swallow the Sun and the Moon, causing solar and lunar eclipse.

Some Days, pp. 13–14

Vatapi be digested: A phrase from the epic, Mahabharata. Two demon brothers, Ilvala and Vatapi, hating Brahmins and sages, schemed to kill them. Vatapi would turn into a goat. Ilvala would then cook the goat and serve it to a Brahmin guest; after the meal, Ilvala would call out, 'Vatapi come out!' And then the demon would burst out of the Brahmin. Hearing of this, Sage Agasthya, went up to the demons' palace and when he was served the meal containing Vatapi, the sage called out, belching, 'Vatapi be digested!' When Ilvala called out 'Vatapi come out', he had already been digested.

Kanigele tree: A black tree that has blood-red flowers.

A Father's gift, p. 16

Supari: Crushed nut from areca palm, a mild narcotic ingredient, for making pan, a chewing quid, containing lime, crushed areca nut, and other ingredients wrapped in a leaf from the betel vines.

On Blast-off and Re-entry, pp. 17–18

Visvarupa: Universal form/shape of the cosmos.
Mohulla: A section or a neighbourhood in a town.

And Now at Midnight, p. 19

Arjuna: The middle brother of the five Pandavas in the epic, Mahabharata. In the poem, the speaker is watching a scene from the epic being enacted at midnight, on a side street in Mysore City.

Uttara: Son of king Virata in the epic Mahabharata. The reference in the poem is to Uttara's shallow and boastful character. Upon facing the enemy he looses his nerve and starts running away from the battlefield. His charioteer Arjuna, in disguise as the eunuch Bruhannale encourages Uttara to live up to his heritage and engage in the battle.

Divine bow: Episode in the Mahabharata. The bow was given to Arjuna by the god Siva.

Khandava: A forest on the banks of the river Yamuna in north India, which the Pandavas received as their moiety when the kingdom was divided, and in it they built their capital, Indraprastha, which is the modern-day Delhi. A mighty fire had to be started to burn the forest. Arjuna and Krishna with the help of the fire god Agni set the forest on fire.

Tonga-wallah: Horse-cart driver.

Arjuna Looks at Draupadi during the Year of Their Disguise, p. 22

In the Mahabharata, the five Pandava brothers and their common wife Draupadi are exiled, and were required to live incognito for one year.

They go to the palace of King Virata and live in disguise without revealing their relationships or identity. The poem imagines, since both Arjuna and Draupadi are in disguise, Arjuna can only make love to her with words.

Kama: God of love.

Jyotirlingam: *Jyoti*: Light; *Lingam*: Phallus. The devotees of Siva believe that there are twelve Jyotirlingas in different parts of India, including Varanasi, Kedar, Srisailam, and Rameshvaram.

In Madhurai, p. 25

Nagamuri flower: The bright flower refers to the lesions on the leper's wounds.

Tali: Wedding chain worn by married women.

Apsaras: Nymphs/Divine women.

Shilpa Shastra: The art/science of sculpture, the smile is according to the thirty-second verse of the *Shilpa Shastra*.

Tribhanga pose: A standing posture in which the figure is curved at the waist and neck to form an 'S' shape.

Khilji: The Khilji dynasty which ruled north India in the twelfth and thirteenth centuries, was the first Muslim power to invade south India. Allauddin Khilji and his commander, Malik Kafur looted many temples and mutilated idols and sculptures.

One of the Five Bhutas, p. 27

Bhutas: Ghosts.

Shanti: Peace.

Panchagavya: Five products of the cow: milk, curds, ghee, urine, cow-dung.

Shraddha ceremony: Ceremony performed for a person who has died.

Bodiless, You, pp. 29–30

Kama: God of love.

Valmiki: Sage, the author of the epic Ramayana. Sage Valmiki once witnessed a hunter killing a bird that was in the act of mating. The cry of the surviving bird angered the sage, and he cursed the hunter. The hunter died instantly. Gods materialized to tell Valmiki that unknowingly he had invented a new meter in creating his curse, and that the curse can be turned into verse to tell the story of Rama and Sita. Valmiki realizing this begins to write the epic, the first stanza of which is the curse itself, which has a double meaning.

Sloka: Verse, couplet, metrical form.

Shunasepa: In the legend of Shunasepa, King Ambarisha undertook a ritual and Indra impounded the ritual's horse. Ambarisha had to exchange a human-animal in lieu of the lost horse, to get it back. When none volunteered, one named Shunasepa, son of Sage Ricika offered himself with a barter of riches to his parents.

Lingam: Phallic emblem associated with the worship of Siva.

Two Eggs, p. 32

When that I was a little tiny boy: From Shakespeare, *Twelfth Night*, V, I.

Mamocked: From Shakespeare, *Coriolanus*, I, iii, 71.

Mohullas in Amritsar: Neighbourhoods in Amritsar, a city in the Punjab.

The Garland of Seasons by Kalidasa: *Ritusamhara* in Haikus, p. 40

Ritusamhara, *The Garland of Seasons* by Kalidasa describes the seasons of the Hindu calendar.

Sampige: Tree with red blooms.

On History, p. 44

Mohammed of Ghor: Invader of north India and the ruler of Afghanistan, conquered north India. He initially suffered setbacks in his battles with Prithviraj Chauhan, the ruler of Delhi, but the latter was finally defeated. He named his slave Kutbuddin Aibak the ruler of Delhi. Shortly thereafter, Aibak became independent and built an iron pillar called the Kutb Minar, a major tourist attraction even today.

Urdu: One of the Indian languages.

Megha Malhar: A melody or musical Raga which is supposed to bring in the rains.

Moghlai masala: A taste for Mughal spices, and other infusions.

Punjab Mail: An express train between Bombay and Peshawar via Delhi. During the partition riots, the train carried refugees from both sides of the border. Each side attacked and about a million people were killed. AKR refers to this in the poem.

To Hayavadana, Our Lord with the Body of a Horse, p. 45

Saint Vadiraja: Belonged to the sect of the Madhva Brahmins of Udipi. He offered food to Hayavadana, god with the body of a horse, by placing a platter of food on his head. The divine horse would approach from behind, placing his forelegs on the Saint's body, and leaving behind the imprint of his hooves on the saint's arms, face, and chest. Madhva Brahmins use sandalwood to mark the hoof prints of a god.

The Body Electric, p. 46

Krittika: The Pleiades, the seven rain stars in the constellation Taurus.

Three Dreams in One Night, p. 47

Sampige-house girl: The girl who lived in the house with the sampige tree with red flowers.

Passing Bells, p. 48

Chinese incident on the border: War with China on the Himalayan border in 1962.

He had to pay a Fine, p. 50

B. M. Shree: (Short for B. M. Sreekantaiya), Kannada poet. In 1926, he published a famous translation of English lyrics (*English Geetegalu*), the first-ever such work in Kannada. BMS is known as the father of twentieth-century Kannada literature. He taught at the University of Mysore. In his book, the opening poem is titled 'Dedication' (*Kanike*), which compares Kannada and English as two lovely women whom he adored. He wished to dress up each girl in the other's costume, to bring out each one's beauty. AKR is amused, but his own two loves rip the borrowed togs off each other's bodies. They will have none of it. The experiment was misunderstood by the watchers, who made him pay for what he tried to do.

Translation, p. 51

Gita (*Bhagavadgita*): In the Mahabharata, before the Kurukshetra battle begins, Arjuna turns to his charioteer, Krishna, (incarnation of Lord Vishnu), with the moral dilemma confronting him: how to kill his relatives and friends. He learns from Krishna that each person must perform his given task and not be concerned about the end result. He must perform his role in life without thoughts of personal gain or loss. People tend to consult the Gita on all matters.

Film Noir, p. 53

Karthika: Here Karthika is a month and not a constellation.
Paste of Neem leaves: A bitter paste from the leaves of the herbal tree 'neem', botanical name, *Azadirachta indica*.

Day's Night, Night's Day, p. 57

Day's Night, Night's Day: The final sentence of this poem is Ramanujan's own addition to a story he has taken from classic Daoism (which later became Zen Buddhism). In the story a man dreams he is a butterfly, and on waking wonders if he is a man or a butterfly dreaming about being a man.

Buddhivanta: a clever man

Not Unlike Dushyanta, p. 58

Dushyanta: Protagonist king in Kalidasa's play *Sakuntala*, based on a few lines in the Mahabharata (II, 67–70). The king's memory of his love for Sakuntala comes back to him only when he sees the ring he had given her. It had fallen off her pining hand, and was later found inside a fish. See AKR's posthumously published short essay, 'The Ring of Memory: Remembering and Forgetting in Indian Literature', in *Uncollected Poems and Prose* (2000).

AND OTHER POEMS

Black into White, p. 63

Jambu Dwipa: In Hindu mythology, Jambu Island is one of the seven continents (or islands) of the world with Mount Meru at its centre.

Jambavanta (or *Jaambavaan*): A monkey leader of extraordinary might from the epic Ramayana.

Vishnu: The god of creation.

Tukaram, Tukaram, p. 67

Tukaram, Tukaram: The seventeenth-century poet saint. A Brahmin is appealing to a non-Brahmin, a Sudra and by intoning his name is able to calm himself; and take a warm bath. *See* E. M. Forster's *A Passage to India*, Ch. 33, where Professor Godbole says: 'Tukaram, Tukaram, Thou art my father and mother and everybody.'

At Night, pp. 68–9

Banavasi: The ancient Kadamba capital and now a small town in the western mountainous region in Karnataka.

Prajavani and *Kannada Prabha*: Names of Kannada newspapers.

A Poison Tree: Poem by William Blake.

Leaves of Grass: Poem by Walt Whitman.

She, p. 70 (also in *SEA*)

Koka Shastra: The science of sex, an ancient manual of sex similar to *Kama Sutra*.

Heard at the School for the Handicapped, p. 73

The teacher and students are stammering.

Karna Kundala: *Karna*: Ear; *Kundala*: Rings, *Karna Kundala*: Name of a flower, associated with spring, with petals that are shaped like loops on earlobes. A play on the words 'ears' and 'springtime flowers'.

Captain Singh's Japanese Dog, p. 74

Annas: Old currency, sixteen annas made one rupee.

Gamester's Dice, p. 76

Mahabharata: Ninth-century BC longest epic. It contains 200,000 couplets. In the dice game mentioned here, Shakuni rolls dice in a game of *pagade*, and the Pandava brothers wager and lose their kingdom and their common wife, Draupadi. The 'Gamester's Dice' draws a parallel between the rolling of the dice in the epic and politics today.

The war in the Mahabharata: The Kaurava and the Pandava brothers engage in a major battle at the end of the Mahabharata.

A Nature-Culture Poem, p. 77

Vibhuti: Holy ash used to place a mark on the forehead.

King Shibi: A dove begged King Shibi for protection from a preying eagle. The eagle said to the king, 'You are depriving me of my food. I will let the dove go, if you will give me an equal share of flesh from your own body.' The king agreed. The eagle made another condition: should the king shed a tear during the operation, the dove would be devoured. The king agreed. Scales were used: the dove sat on one side and the king's flesh was placed on the other. But no matter how much of the king's body was taken out, the dove continued to be heavier. Finally, the king himself sat on one side of the scale to see if he could balance the weight of the dove. The gods were testing King Shibi. Then the eagle and the dove vanished, and in their place stood Dharmaraj, the king of righteousness, and Indra, the king of the heavens. King Shibi had passed the ultimate test of sacrifice. The poet uses the allusion to underline what goes on in our own times.

Dis-Ease, p. 80

Neti: For nasal irrigation.

Sampige flowers: (Campaka in Sanskrit); Blossoms of various colours from the tree *Michelia campaka*

A Million Points of Light, p. 81

Bodhisattva Avalokileswara: Painting from the Gupta period, 4th–5th century AD, Ajanta Caves.

Paramahansa Said, pp. 82–3

Paramahansa: Hindu Bengali mystic who taught tolerance and secularism.

Devi: Distinct from consort goddesses, Devi is part of the folk mythology.

Yellow turmeric rice: Rice mixed with turmeric is considered holy (auspicious) and used during worship.

Vermilion (Kumkum): Red powder women wear in the middle of their forehead.

Kumkum rice: Rice mixed with vermilion powder.

Neem leaf: Bitter leaf from a tree, used as an ingredient in a variety of herbal remedies; *Azadivachta indica*.

Black puja: Prayer ritual performed by a sorcerer.

Durga: Hindu Goddess.

Lotus Position: A yogic sitting posture.

Satyam Shivam Sundaram, p. 84

The title, literally means beauty is truth, beauty is god.

The Two Wristwatches, p. 86

Bangalore: A south Indian city.

America, Our Common Future, p. 87

Namums: Vertical marks worn by traditional Brahmins and other worshippers of Vishnu.

Twice-born men: Brahmins are the highest of the three twice-born castes; born once at birth, and the second time at their initiation, when they are invested with the sacred thread.

The Yamuna: River in north India.

The sacred Ganga: Hindus consider all rivers as holy, and the Ganga is one of the holiest.

From pavilions in Mahabharata: Blowing of the conch was a tradition during battles, both to celebrate victory, and to convey messages to the soldiers.

The conch shell becomes a musical instrument: After the mollusks in them die, the larger conch shells are used as musical instruments, particularly during prayers and ceremonies.

Rama's Feast Day: The ninth day of the bright fortnight of the month of Caitra (March–April), Lord Rama's birthday, a major festival.

Have I not Said, p. 89 (also in *SEA*)

Talkadu: A town in Karnataka.

Dosa: Pancake made from rice and lentils.

Pan: Areca nut, lime, etc., wrapped in betel leaf, for chewing.

Kumkum: Red auspicious sign (vermilion) worn by women on their foreheads.

On Music, p. 90

Krishna–Radha: Radha is Lord Krishna's consort; the two are deemed to be the ideal couple.

Tribute to Ho Chi Minh (to Nguyen That Thanh, Ho Chi Minh), p. 93

Nguyen That Thanh, Ho Chi Minh: Hero of Vietnam. He was born with the name Nguyen That Thanh and later assumed his more famous name, Ho Chi Minh. He wrote these poems while he was incarcerated in a Chinese prison. Ramanujan's specific source for these poems is not known.

Main Attraction: Bald-Headed Eagle in the Museum, p. 94

At the Maharaja's palace: During the fall festival of Dussehra, the palace in Mysore (south India) is decorated with tens of thousands of lights.

Grandfather, p. 97

Bangles: Glass or plastic bracelets.

A Question, pp. 99–100

Ayyo: An exclamation meaning, 'Oh, My!'

Gurus made the children stand on their heads: Rigorous discipline enforced by teachers on their pupils in olden days.

Golden Age: Reference to the prosperous period during the reign of the kings of the Vijayanagara dynasty in south India in the fifteenth century.

Laxmi: Goddess of wealth, Vishnu's consort.

Kerala: A state in south-west India.

Harijans: The untouchables of India were called Harijans or people of God, by Mahatma Gandhi.

Brahmin's well: The well in a Brahmin's house is considered pure, and the untouchables were forbidden to go near it.

Nazis making lampshades: Nazis are said to have used body parts like bones and skin from mass graves for making soap, lampshades, and the like.

In Mysore, You Speak It, pp. 102–3 (Also in *SEA*)

Chitragupta: The bookkeeper for Yama, the god of death.
Kabuli Madam: Belly dancer in Kabul, capital of Afghanistan.

In Transit p. 104

Kathmandu: Capital of Nepal.
Hunsur: A town in Karnataka state, India.
Ganesha Bidis: Bidis are rolled tobacco in leaves, smoked as cigarettes. Ganesha Bidi is a popular commercial brand of bidi.
Lord Krishna's feast day: The birth anniversary of Lord Krishna, the eighth day of the dark fortnight in the month of Bhadra (August–September).
Hare Krishna: Modern Hare Rama Hare Krishna movement.

Cave Paintings, p. 105

The cave paintings in Bhopal, 20,000 years old.

Flying with the Wings of Bees, p. 107

Yayati: King in the Mahabharata. For snubbing the daughter of an ascetic guru, he is cursed with old age. He is given a reprieve: he could exchange the curse with another person. Not finding anyone willing to exchange his old age with his youth, he succeeds in exchanging his decrepitude with the glowing youth of his own son, Puru.
Chamundi: Goddess with six arms.
'*And as our poet said: Let us fly with the wings of bees*' and '*O sister, have you seen the gossamer wings of moths?*': The lines are from D. R. Bendre (1896–1981).

Black is the Shadow of What is Invisible, p. 111

Jules Fernand Leger (1881–1955): French painter, founder of the Cubist movement.

Non-fiction, p. 113

Malli: The girl with the lamp, is the shade of the man's wife.

In Passing, p. 114

Rahu: At the churning of the oceans, a demon, appeared in the guise of a god to receive the divine nectar (amrita) which gives immortality. The sun and the moon warned Lord Vishnu, who then split the demon's body, but since the demon had partaken of the divine drink and had become immortal, Vishnu allowed the head and tail to survive in the heavens as Rahu and Ketu. They swallow the sun and the moon, causing solar and lunar eclipses.

Primeval bed of the universal Lord, *Vishnu*: Vasuki, a gigantic snake with a thousand heads in the primeval ocean forms a coil-like mattress, on which the god Vishnu sleeps. Lord Vishnu is the preserver of the entire universe.

Beyond the Brushwood, pp. 115–16

Mirza-plant: A thorny weed.

Angel's Trumpet: Long-stemmed flowers of the *Datura* plant (source of belladonna).

Ganja: Marijuana, genus *cannabis*.

I Believe, p. 118

Mohulla: A neighbourhood in a city.

Kama Sutra: Ancient sex manual.

Casanova: The famous eighteenth-century womanizer from Italy.

All Too Often When, p. 119

Pushpaka: A mythical airplane, light as a flower, in which Lord Rama and his wife Sita flew.

During the War in Vietnam, p. 120

In Saigon: The self-immolation of a monk in yellow robes, captured on film as it happened, and shown on TV the world over, became a famous icon of protest, during the war in Vietnam.

In the Sixties, p. 121

Garlic sambar: Vegetable stew with spices and garlic.

American Vatapi and *Vatapi be digested*: Refer to Vatapi and Ilvala, two demon brothers in the epic Mahabharata. Hating Brahmins and sages, and scheming to kill and eat them, Vatapi would turn into a goat and Ilvala would then cook the goat and serve it to Brahmin guests; after the meal, Ilvala would call out, 'Vatapi come out!', and then the demon would burst out of the Brahmin. Hearing of this, Sage Agasthya went up to the demons' palace, and when he was served the meal containing Vatapi, the sage called out, belching, 'Vatapi be digested!' When Ilvala called out, 'Vatapi come out', he had already been digested.

Somehow Somewhere, p. 123

Bandra: A suburb in greater Bombay (Mumbai).

Our Cat Tiger, p. 124 (also in *SEA*)

Another Ramanujan: Saint Ramanujan founder of the Brahmin sect of Visishtadvaita.

Back on Terra Firma, pp. 125–6

The dharma of convenience: Minor compromises one makes in the practice of ethical principles and guidelines.

Nagaland: A state in north-eastern India.

KUNTOBILLE

Hopscotch, p. 130

Visvarupa: Form/shape of the cosmos.

Old House Revisited, p. 132

Rupees: Indian currency.

Mahut: The elephant keeper/rider.

Twin Birds of the Upanishads, p. 133

Upanishads: Religious texts, starting 700 BC, the simile of the two birds is from the *Mundaka Upanishad*. The two birds stand for the watching self, and the acting self.

The Ekka Plant, p. 135

Ekka Plant: Plant of the Devil, ash-smeared bud, and tumid bloom.

The Ekka oozes a gummy milk: The Ekka is a wild plant that has long fat flowers, thick coarse leaves; it oozes sticky white when torn; children like to break the leaf, pull it apart bit by bit, to collect the thick sap, to make a thin film with the juice, so as to see their own reflection in it, or to watch the colours that appear in sunlight.

A Poem by Anna Akhmatova, p. 137

A translation of Anna Akhmatova's 'Imitation from the Armenian', which opens with the line, 'I will appear in your dreams as a black ewe,' *The Complete Poems of Anna Akhmatova*, tr. by Judith Hemschemeyer (Zephyr Press, Boston) p. 665, reproduced here.

An Enchanted Flute, p. 138

After Rainer Maria Rilke's *Sonnets to Orpheus*, Part One, Sonnet 1:1. Translation by David Young, *Sonnets to Orpheus* (Wesleyan University Press, Middleton, Connecticut, 1987).

As cowherd Krishna: In mythology, Lord Krishna, as a cowherd, plays divine music from his enchanting flute, which attracts cows and women.

For Some, p. 144

Pongal: festival of spring; also festival of cattle.
Muhammed of Ghazni: The tenth-century Muslim ruler from Ghazni province in Afghanistan, who invaded India seventeen times and sacked cities and capitals, destroying Buddhist, Jain, and Hindu idols and temples.

A Reel Played Over and Over, p. 145

Mysore: Mysore city, south India.
Neem toothpaste: a popular brand of toothpaste containing the bitter extract of the neem, an indigenous medicinal tree.

The River, p. 149

Town of burning ghats: Varanasi, a city in north India where cremations are conducted on the banks of the river Ganga, a holy city for Hindus.

Drinking Gin, p. 150

Ahiramruga: Imaginary animal with two serpent heads and the trunk of a deer.

When in Your Mind You Are, p. 152

Rakshasa: Mythical demon.

1940 Perhaps, p. 156

Doddathe: Mother's or father's elder sister, or father's or mother's elder brother's wife.
Appa and Amma: Father and mother.

Reason for Not Composing Sun and Moon Poems, p. 157

Bidi: A cigarette of rolled tobacoo leaf, without filter or paper.

Inscape, p. 162

The Vedantic spread: Vedanta texts. Vedanta literally means end of the Vedas. It is one of the six orthodox systems of Indian philosophy and includes the Upanishads, the *Brahmasutras*, and the Bhagavadgita, along with commentaries of these texts.

On Tenali Rama's Gesture as a New Interpretation of the Ramayana, p. 165

Tenali Rama: Comedian, jester in the court of King Krishnadevaraya of Vijayanagar in the sixteenth century. In the poem, Tenali Rama's gesture is seen as a new interpretation of the epic, Ramayana.

The Ramayana: Ancient Indian epic.

Bound and Flayed, p. 167

Poet Valmiki: Sage, author of the epic, Ramayana. Valmiki once witnessed a hunter killing a bird that was in the act of mating. The cry of the surviving bird angered the sage, and he cursed the hunter. The hunter died instantly. Gods materialized to tell Valmiki that unknowingly he had invented a new meter in uttering his curse. Valmiki went on to use the same meter to write the story of Rama and Sita. He began his epic with the curse itself, which he realized had a double meaning.

Sabari: A devotee of Rama in the Ramayana. Born of low caste, she lived in the deep forest of Dandaka hoping that someday Lord Rama would arrive at her hut and bless her. She waited for a number of years for that moment of benediction. Eventually Rama appeared, and received her humble hospitality.

Personae, p. 168

Nirodh: A brand of condoms.

On Crying, p. 171

Written after reading a few lines by Josephine Jacobson. *See* 'Tears' by Josephine Jacobson, in *In the Crevice of Time, New and Collected Poems* (John Hopkins University Press, Baltimore) pp. 249–50.

Mohenjo-Daro: The site of a prehistoric civilization in north-west India (now in Pakistan).

An Uncommonly Common Man, p. 172

St Vemana: A fifteenth-century mystic, Telugu poet, and philosopher, who wrote thousands of couplets dealing with living an ethical life of devotion.

Mangalsutra: Chain worn by married women, the equivalent of a wedding ring.

On Quests, pp. 174–5

Koh-i-noor: A diamond that was in the possession of the kings of central India, Mughal emperors, the Persian invader Nadir Shah, and the Sikh king of Punjab, Ranjit Singh, before it fell into the hands of the British in 1849. It was presented to Queen Victoria in 1851 and remains in the possession of the British royal family, in spite of the efforts by India to get it back.

Nalanda: City in the state of Bihar, north India; a famous centre of Buddhist learning, with monasteries; considered one of the world's oldest residential universities.

Internal Ganga: The river Ganga is considered holy; *Antarganga* or internal Ganga refers to insight and wisdom, or the flow of consciousness.

On Mahavira's Story, p. 176

The Kannada text claims that this image was suggested by (an image in) Brecht.

O Lord, Whether *You* Exist or Not, pp. 179–82

Alwars: Vaisnava devotional poets from the Tamil regions. The word, alwars, literally means, 'Drowning in You'.

Vedanta: Literally means end of the Vedas. It is one of the six orthodox systems of Indian philosophy and includes the Upanishads, the *Brahmnasutras* and the Bhagavadgita, along with commentaries on these texts.

Cupola: The temple's silent bell.

Supari: Crushed areca nut; ingredient of pan used for after-dinner chewing; addictive.

Neempaste applied to the nipples: Bitter paste from the medicinal herb, neem, applied to the nipples to wean a breastfeeding child.

Marana, Sarana, p. 184

Marana, sarana: Marana means death; sarana means a devotee of Shiva, or one who surrenders. Marana/Sarana means: Death/Surrender. The Kannada title was: 'Naked Prayer, Another Tradition'.

But hunger took him by surprise: Is after a line by Terry Campbell in 'Thanksgiving Rhyme' ('Hunger took the humans by surprise').

Brahma Jnana: A Silent Sonnet, p. 186

This page offers the metrical pattern of a silent sonnet.

Jnana: Knowledge; *Brahma*: Godhead.

Book Two: A Novella
Someone Else's Autobiography

Someone Else's Autobiography

by

A. K. RAMANUJAN

CONTENTS

A Mock Memoir

In Ramanujan's novella, *Someone Else's Autobiography*, two expatriates, a history teacher, K. K. Ramanujan, and a poet, A. K. Ramanujan, meet by chance in Chicago. KKR tells AKR that he is on a quest in search of himself: he feels displaced, misplaced, and incomplete. The poet advises the historian to write it all down, to help him find his lost self. This advice is along the same lines as taking the 'talking cure'. When the historian sends his personal history to the poet, chapter by chapter, AKR responds to the instalments, with cryptic remarks or with mock-serious verses. In this way, the poet becomes the mentor to the historian.

This novella owes something to the idea of doppelgangers, but the doubles in it tell stories. One notices that their stories have unusual obsessions that on closer reading turn out to be uncommonly connected to the themes running through the whole work. In structure, the stories fit one into the next, like a set of Indian boxes, the larger one accommodating the smaller. There are frames within frames, stories within stories. They all seem to be about the search for the self, or search for the invisible line where the self ends and where *someone else* begins.

Literally and metaphorically, the core of the narrative comes out of the idea of twinning. In a surprising way, the author connects the idea of *doubles* with twinning, of being literally a twin. The lack of boundary between the self and the other comes out of the life lived in India, in the family, and in the community.

Even though a portion of the novella is set in the US, the narrator in the outer frame of the story has yet to leave India. His thesis is that we each have an embryonic twin embedded in us. Or as in the case of the Siamese twins in Chapter 19, some of us are joined at the hip, and each has to wait patiently while the other is answering nature, enjoying physical pleasure, or dying. The characters are, sometimes, interchangeably succubus and incubus. KKR, the narrator and his wife lose the sense of who is what through merger, each accuses the other of being a plagiarist. They become psychophages, devouring each other's psyches.

KKR complains that too many individuals carry the same name. (Unlike Edgar Allan Poe's story of doubles with the same name, William Wilson, the confusion in *SEA* is about the familiar first names.) The first name—Ramu—belongs to several persons in KKR's extended family. It is also shared by the author, who in real life, was known as Ramu to his family. Since KKR's 'autobiography' is *someone else's*, we cannot assume that it is a straightforward confession.

Furthermore, the narrator's first erotic experience is with an acacia tree; he does not know the difference between a man and a woman, between a sibling and a stranger, between his own writing self and that of others. He is an absurdist. He mistakes a post office clerk to be his illegitimate sister, he thinks the sounds in the house at night are proof that he has an unacknowledged brother who visits only at night; and he assumes the brother has been sent away to Africa. Once KKR arrives in the US, his interest is perked when he encounters anyone from Africa, in the hope of finding out about his phantom brother.

The realistic outer frame of the narrative, concerns the three days when KKR is in his mid-teens: he goes with his father to Madras, to visit a dying relative. In appearance, the father is a sort of Professor Godbole, an interesting mixture of East and West; he wears a turban, tootal ties, muslin dhoti, and tweed jackets. This is an accurate description of the author's own father, Srinivas Iyengar.

The narrator's mother is a second wife, haunted by the ghost of the first wife. All the characters, including the mother and father, tell their stories to KKR.

The novella ends with KKR's recognition of his father's unique unflappable unassailable Brahmanic sense of self. To the reader, this is a contrast to the incompleteness of the narrator who sees himself as half a person, caught between the hunger for individuation and the anxiety caused by merging with someone else.

In writing a memoir, KKR glimpses the self in the other, and the other in the self. In his interaction with AKR, he, the prose writer, finds the poet in himself and his alter ego, the poet, finds the prose writer in himself. In spite of the Naipaulian sidereal scenes in the novella, there is recognition at the end.

The novella is a mock autobiography. It uses the autobiographical technique to ponder on certain ideas relating to: who am I? Is this an Indian preoccupation? The narrative seems to run along, associationally, and contains unforgettable episodes from the writer's notebook.

In hunting for a self, the narrator seems to have found his self, as well as his anti-self. In this modern poet's imaginings, the Keatsian *negative capability* is compounded with the Yeatsian 'mirror-resembling' idea, and it is filtered through T. S. Eliot's hand-me-down lens: '*mon semblable—mon frère*'.

Shouri Daniels-Ramanujan
Northfield, MN, USA

Chapter One

The Three Days

1953. I was seventeen then. No, perhaps it was 1957. I went to Madras[†] with Appa for three days. That was my first trip with him, just the two of us, and it turned out to be the last. Appa's sister, Atthe,[†] sent a postcard to say that her husband was gravely ill; his belly had been swollen for months, and there was no relief in sight.

It's strange. I don't know why, but for five or six months, the events of our three days in Madras still haunt me. From twenty years ago and so far away, all the little details continue to prey on me: my aunt's face in her dimly lit Georgetown[†] annex, the flashing diamonds in her necklace, her earrings, her nose rings. The roar of the sea, the smell of the Madras beach, the sound of the surf are with me this Minnesota autumn, here, where no street or tree or bird has a familiar name, where the food, the faces, and the inflections are foreign to me.

I thought, if I could write about it, I might put to rest my pursuing demons. I had no skill in writing about such things, that too in Kannada;[†] my fingers seemed frozen, until just the other day.

Chapter Two

The Other Man

Truth itself is strange, and as they say in English, stranger than fiction. A curious thing happened the other day.

I went from Bloomington to Chicago, where I happened to meet a man. Strange to say, he had the same name as I, my very own name. He was A. K. Ramanujan. I am K. K. Ramanujan. Just a single letter to mark our difference. His middle school Kannada teacher used to taunt him, 'ÁéKé?' as if each syllable of his name was under review. In the same way my friend Narasimayya Murthy used to torment me by giggling and saying, 'KéKé?' As you can see, both were low-level wits.

After wandering here and there, this other man, A. K. Ramanujan, found a job in Chicago to teach Kannada and Tamil[†] to Americans. He even boasted that he was a Kannada poet.

As I said, the encounter seemed strange to me. He was ten years older than I and wore gold-rimmed glasses. Like me, he had been living in America for many years. Until 1950, his mother's house was in Mysore[†] on a street near D. Subbayya Road, he said. My mother still lives there; I thought, Amma might even know his mother.

When he heard my name, he was as surprised as I was upon hearing his.

'What do they call you at home?' he said.

'Ramu,' I said.

'They called me "Ramu" too in Mysore, and over here, "Raman" has become my new nickname,' he said.

'I was "Ramanja" in Mysore and "Ram" here; some even call me

"Mr Raymon John". For Americans who have been to India, I am "Ramanoojan,"' I said.

He seemed relieved to find at least some difference between us. Still, we were both uneasy about such close parallels between us.

That reminds me of what I heard at a beer party. One man said, 'Don't think that you and I, and our planet earth are unique in the universe. Over there, in that boundless sky, there are innumerable suns. Around each sun, there are countless worlds, planets, moons—many a Mars and many a Venus.'

Then a sceptical voice said, 'That's just fantasy, make-believe; it's Flash Gordon and Star Wars. A steady fare of science fiction will do that for you. Think about it: on those planets, there's no air or light. No greenery or life-sustaining water. All are barren. Man went to the moon and back, and what did he find there? A handful of moon rocks! Only on this earth, life has evolved, by chance no doubt.'

The first speaker said, 'Man, let me tell you something. Not only are there planets like our own, it is most likely there are people just like us in the universe. Men with similar names, people in similar bodies, wearing similar clothes, sitting in front of a table just like this one, perhaps arguing over the same subject, at this very moment! It is not only a possibility, it is a probability.'

When I think such thoughts, I break into a cold sweat. I hold onto a chair, or stare at faces; I look into eyes, I see nose hairs sticking out and such, and I pinch myself saying, 'This is real too. Real. I am real! I am not an illusion.'

That is exactly how I felt on meeting A. K. Ramanujan, but the difference was this: the longer I stared at him, the more my fancy took hold of me; and yet, I knew that he was different from me in age, complexion, body build, height, and weight. We were born in different towns, we grew up differently, and we came to America in different years, through different means. My wife Joanie is American. I teach American and Indian history in a small Iowa college, and I don't know much about Kannada literature; his interests are language and literature, not history.

Even so, we came from the same Iyengar Brahmin[†] community; we were both raised near D. Subbayya Road; we had the same names, and many of our friends had the same names, and we both had a friend called Ratna. Our parents were from Madras. I had to pinch myself, and repeat, 'No, no! He is not me. His mind, his physical self, and his personal history are all different from mine.' Still, my unique separate identity was again in question.

I saw that he had a habitual obsession. Just moments after meeting me, he said, 'Do you write?'

'A couple of papers, yes, on the history of Mysore, about Tippu Sultan',[†] I said.

'You must write an autobiography. There are so many Indians here, in this country, but no one has written an autobiography of any depth. You are even married to an American! All of America is like an in-law's home to you.' His laughter became high-pitched. I said, 'Ayyo![†] I don't know how to write stories. My Kannada is poor; I have not found anyone who speaks Kannada here. I'm even forgetting my own language.'

'That's the very reason why a person in your situation must write. (Yet I must say, when writers attempt to create "literature", it becomes contrived, full of artifice. Let me insist: a poem ought not to poeticize, a drama must not be too theatrical.) If you keep writing, your Kannada will come back to you. Just go ahead and write!' He held forth on the subject of writing, saying, 'Keep sending me what you write. I know people in Bangalore[†] and Dharwar;[†] we'll get it published.' He was bragging again, and I was tempted.

'I have thought of writing, but found no reason for it. The only story I know is my own story,' I said.

'That's so with all of us! We know one story. Our own. Some of us write them as "stories" and change the names of people and places, while others write them as "autobiographies", that's all! I don't have to teach you. After all, you are a man of history! Just go ahead and write. Don't give it a second thought.'

'I'll try, if you'll correct my Kannada?'

'Yes, yes. What is there to correct? As they say, "Wherever an elephant walks, there's a road; whatever a Kannada man writes, there's Kannada."' Spouting proverbs, he took down my address. About four days later, I received in the mail a poem he had written. A vulgar poem. Read just the first four lines and skip the rest.

In Mysore
You speak it
In America
You write it
As verse
There may be
Pure cream
In a man's home
But he is not
Tempted
Some men are
Like that
When they find
Their one-eyed-one
Slumbers and
Will not rise
For wedded wife
Dejected he may
Enter his name in
Chitragupta's[†]
Register of death
To change from
Slithering snake
To walking Elephant
To crawling turtle
Flat and frigid
He asks, O Kama[†]

Is apathy
My karma?
A thousand
Miles from home
In a Kabuli[†]
Madam's den
Among wiggling
Veiled belly dancers
Memory of his
Bedded wife becomes
His aphrodisiac

Chapter Three

The Letter in a Bottle

Until the other day, I was not even sure if I could write anything like this. That too, sitting here, in Winona, Minnesota, some 10,000 miles away, I couldn't have known that I would be writing in the spoken Kannada of Mysore, where I was born thirty-eight years ago, or that I would write anything like this in the common everyday words of both ministers and peons, using the language they used when quarrelling or coughing or dreaming.

Shouldn't there be a reason for a story? For whom should one write? An American lad once placed his picture in a bottle with a note inside: 'If you receive this, please write me back at this address.' He sealed the bottle with wax and set it afloat on the Atlantic. Ten years later he received a reply from a girl in England, 'I got your note and found the address in the bottle.' He went in search of her, found her, and even married her. Should I write hoping for such a reader? In Kannada? Sitting here? I am reminded of the man who took a stranger's advice and stood on the shore, his mouth full of pebbles, trying to deliver a speech across the Atlantic as a cure for his stuttering.

Yet, there are many reasons for writing in one's mother tongue. A Romanian friend, who like me married an American woman, writes all his personal stories in Romanian, not in English. He is afraid that his wife might look at it. He wrote in Romanian not out of love for his mother tongue but to enable people in his own country, 6,000 miles away, to read what he wrote, freely and openly, whether true or fictitious, about his wife and about his girlfriends. But where he lives, no one can read his book, not even the persons whom he has written about. See the irony!

Chapter Four

Further Reasons for Writing

My Telugu friend Viswamithra, who roomed with me during our studies in Champaign, had different reasons for writing than my Romanian friend. Each night Viswamithra wrote steamy stories of his love in a black notebook—not in English, but in Telugu, so that his wife, who lived in Vishakhapattanam,[†] India, with their three children, could read it the next year. He had a peculiar sense of being faithful. He adopted many American habits. His clothes, car, tennis shoes, the under-arm spray deodorant, the three kinds of hair rinses, the medicine for heartburn, and the aspirin he carried in his pocket for headaches made me think of him as the most Americanized Indian I have known. The first thing he did in his office each day was to pick up from his desktop, a studio photograph of his wife and children taken in India. He would then wipe it clean with a napkin, and like Americans, he would place it on the desk, right next to a photograph of his American girlfriend.

One midnight as I stayed up studying for the next day's Russian history test, I heard Viswamithra coming in, noisily stomping the heels of his shoes to get rid of the snow. He then banged the door open, entered with a blast of cold air, slamming the door shut. He seemed to be in a state.

'Viswa, did you drive far? What's the matter?' I asked him in English.

Viswamithra was named after an ancient sage. (Viswamithra in Champaign, Illinois! His brothers too had mythological names like Ambarisha,[†] Vedavyasa.[†]) He could get high with a single bottle of beer. Had he drunk two bottles, I wondered. Had his *Brahmarandhra*[†] burst open sprouting a thousand lotuses? I could only speculate, looking at his blood-shot eyes.

'Oh, nothing. Just fifty miles. I went to Motamb...,' he stopped.

I guessed where he had been. To Susan's place. The American girlfriend whose picture graced his desk. Two years ago she gave him a kiss. Months later at a party, after getting drunk, he returned that kiss while bidding her goodnight. That intoxication has not dimmed even after two years. Certainly, three beers could not have given him such a high; he was like one who, when experimenting with drugs for the first time, has taken too much LSD. His world turned upside down. The earth, the chairs, the faces, the trees, the fingers, his dead sister's hands, twinkling rhinestones in the glass chandelier, everything swirled into a thousand colours. The grand illusion lasted two whole days. Dormant feelings of this kind might suddenly burst forth years later, when least expected: perhaps, while taking a piss off a road in Germany or Mysore, or while looking at the iridescence of piss, or while noticing the gleam in the eyes reflected in a bathroom mirror. To the dismay of one's wife and children, such unsettling confusions are likely to linger for hours and days. For Viswamithra, the memory of Susan's kiss was like that, its tumult rising off and on, shattering our sage's peace of mind and upsetting his daily routines.

'How was it?' I asked him again in English.

'Oh, today I died,' he said.

'What do you mean? What happened?'

'Oh, nothing. Susie let me sleep with her,' he said, sighing, as if unable to contain his agitation.

'Oh, poor man! You had to wait so many years for this. Congratulations,' I said.

I heard another sigh, followed by silence.

'Aren't you happy?' I said.

'Didn't I say, I died?' he said.

He sighed again, and was silent. Viswamithra did not speak for two days.

During those two days, he wrote in his black book. As soon as he came home, he would stomp his heels to get the snow off, and he would start writing. He wrote on the toilet, he wrote in bed before he fell asleep, he wrote in bed upon waking. He wrote in Telugu so that his wife could read all of it in Vishakhapattanam the next year.

To this day I do not know what exactly transpired between Viswamithra and Susie that night. Did he finally sleep with her, or did he find out that he couldn't get it up, and so, was he ashamed of the shutdown? Or, did she allow him to sleep next to her, but more like an infant next to its mother, and did she caress his graying hair and advise him lovingly, 'Please Vish, from now on, don't come here. Think of your wife and children.' Or, did he see a blemish on her skin, a scar on her belly and lose interest, turning into an ascetic sage like Vemana[†] of his motherland. I do not know to this day.

On a couple of occasions during those two days, I tried to steal a look at his diary and flipped the pages of his black book. The serpentine Telugu script written in jet-black ink filled page after page. His writing was a tangled string of scorpion claws. The Telugu script looked like Kannada, but I could not read it. Seeing the familiar script, half-familiar words, and completely unfamiliar sentences, I found no answers to my puzzles. I was disappointed. I felt like kicking myself.

From that day on, Viswamithra stopped getting drunk on beer, concentrated on his PhD, worked on his thesis day and night. He wrote, tore what he wrote, rewrote what he had torn away, and wrote again. His subject was statistics. He measured, he diagrammed; numbers and graphs became the language of his dreams. He prepared bell-shaped graphs and Chamundi Hill[†]-shaped graphs, diagrams looking like a street with a slope. He completed his thesis in just three months, had it typed, made us proofread it and we caught typos. He arranged the pages in neat stacks, had them bound, submitted his dissertation, earned his doctorate, gave a beer party, and went away to see his wife and children. He packed his four black books carefully, along with his camera and the tape recorder, and securely locked the suitcase. Within a radius of hundreds of miles of Champaign, Illinois, there would not have been a single person who could have read his Telugu notebooks, but what Viswamithra wrote was meant for the eyes of none other than his other half. Ratna wrote to me the other day that Viswamithra now has two more children.

Chapter Five

A Brother and a Sister

He asked me to write a personal history. When I began, what I wrote was well focused, but then it started meandering into this, that, and the other thing. When you start writing, sometimes your dates get muddled; sometimes, simple questions go unanswered. When I tell you my story, shouldn't I, the narrator, have mother, father, brothers, sisters; and shouldn't I be writing about them?

I have either two or three brothers, and two or three sisters. When I write it down that way, you may be thinking: 'Did he say two, or did he say three? Doesn't he know how to count? We are in some trouble here.'

Well, here is why. As far as I know, I have two brothers, Gopi, fifty-three, and Venkatesha, forty-five. But since childhood, I have suspected that somewhere I have another brother, the eldest of all. It could be that he worked all day and came home at night after I fell asleep. This would account for the strange sounds I sometimes heard in the middle of the night: doors slamming, chairs and tables being moved, a bed squeaking near my father's room, and whispers. Those sounds could have been made by the comings and goings of the brother I did not know. I sometimes think that he quarrelled with Appa and Amma when he was younger and ran away to Africa. I kept feeling that I had a big brother who was taking care of me from far away. As for Gopi, he and I rarely talked; he was seldom in town. Once, when I was six and Venkatesha was fourteen, I was distressed that Gopi was not letting me join them for cricket. I almost said to them, 'Just wait and see; I'll tell our big brother!'

One day, when I was eight, I took an album from Amma's cupboard, and for an entire hour, looked through it, leaning across her rolled-up bed. Her bed carried the smell of her body; I found some crushed jasmine petals from her hair in its folds. In that album there were photographs of family members, snapshots from when they were young. The picture of my dead aunt showed her in a role from the play Ashadabhuti.[†] She wore white ash stripes on her dark face and forearms. Her long hair was plaited and hidden under a man's turban. And then there were pictures of Appa and my uncles: photographs of them in turbans; faded pictures of four black-robed men at their graduation holding rolled-up BA diplomas; photographs of them sitting in front of a flower-painted screen; and so on. There was one photograph of a stranger—a man with a mustache, in a military uniform, holding a military baton, standing in style.

Amma never answered my questions about him. 'Oh, him! He is the son of our uncle's first wife. He went away to Africa or somewhere, during the Hitler War.' Africa again! Just as I thought.

'Where is he now?' I asked.

'He has gone somewhere... Let's see... How many years have passed? Who knows where he is? Why do you want to know about these things? Why is this picture in the album? We should get rid of it.' She yanked the album from my hands but the picture was never taken out.

I had my doubts, and to hear their private conversation on the subject, I often hid in the corners of the room, but neither Appa nor Amma revealed any clues concerning that mysterious military man. I believed that he, this brother of mine, would someday suddenly spring from the earth to save me from an impending disaster, just as Dr Zhivago's brother did in the novel. I often wondered how my brother would look; could he have been any one of the many passers-by? I imagined his appearance by adding twenty years to the photograph in the album, adding a tiny bit of gray over there, a bald spot over here, and a belly-bulge in the middle.

By the time I was fourteen or fifteen, I had forgotten all this. But, when I came to America, perhaps out of fear or loneliness, these thoughts resurfaced, and when I was with students or friends from Africa, I even made covert inquiries about him. This may sound crazy, but an anxiety or an unsettled feeling of having seen someone somewhere has remained with me. Now that I am thirty-seven, this notion is no longer persistent, though it lingers somewhere at the back of my mind.

It is a different matter about my other sister. Ever since I was twelve, I knew that besides the two sisters at home, I had a third one, Appa's daughter, living elsewhere! I even know her name, but I won't tell you; there is no need to reveal it. Still, I could not have imagined that Appa was that kind of man.

Although Amma and Appa drew closer to each other in later years, once in a while I felt that a glass wall existed between them, as in their sudden silences in the middle of a casual conversation.

'Do you know…yesterday our old friend from Tumkur[†] came to the office?' Appa said one day.

'Who? Gopalaraya? The one who won thirty-six thousand rupees wagering a mere four-anna bet?' Amma said.

Of all the persons I knew he was the only one who won thousands of rupees from the lotteries. Thereafter he was 'Lottery Gopalaraya'.

'Yes, him. He and I studied at Madras Christian College, Tamaram,'[†] Appa said.

'Don't I know!' Amma said, and suddenly she stopped talking and went into the kitchen pretending to check if the rice was cooked. Even in the heat of the kitchen, I felt a sudden chill.

'Oh, you! You never believe what I say; you're so suspicious,' Appa said.

'Stop! Don't talk about it now. The children are up,' Amma said, sounding as if she was hissing between sealed lips. I looked around. Clearly I was the only 'child' there. Father gulped his coffee and walked away. An hour later he came back, as if nothing had happened. That night, he spread out a mat and played pagade[†] using yellow dice. He lost.

The girl they were referring to was probably my eldest sister. She seemed to be about five or six years older than Kamali and Sumithrini. Her eyes, nose, parting of hair resembled theirs. I have seen her in Mysore; her mother taught in a school. The girl was dark and tall with an unsmiling face, and she sold stamps in Ontikoppal† post office. Just about then women were beginning to find office jobs. I think she was not married. Certainly she seemed to know who I was and I knew that she knew from the way she behaved, avoiding a direct gaze, trying to steal a glance when my back was turned. Her pinched nose and facial features were like Appa's. Once when I purposely went to see her in Ontikoppal post office and pretended to buy stamps, she was startled, and I got away quickly. I never went there again.

I wondered whether Appa knew about her, whether he was still romancing her mother on the side; I wondered if there was a hidden passage in his otherwise tidy 'bourgeois' life. I also wondered whether I had more brothers and sisters in other towns, and, if so, where how when, and whether Amma knew all this and endured it with forbearance. The puzzling doubts and questions persisted. When I returned home from Ontikoppal I was very agitated and anxious to investigate these matters further. I wanted to question all of them directly: the woman at the post office, Amma, Appa. My opinion about them had changed completely. I was scared. I couldn't trust anyone in Ontikoppal. I was twelve then. The year was 1951.

If this were a fictitious story, I would have had to take care of this problem and provide a satisfactory ending, but this being a true story, these matters cannot be neatly resolved. Although the puzzles have faded somewhat, every now and then they reappear. A story has no feet, but truth walks away. That which happened is the truth, and usually told in the simple past tense, but history is in motion; it is best told as a serial to be continued.

It marches on, using its own feet. It is customary to use the past tense when referring to true stories, but history is in motion; it is best told in the present continuous.

Chapter Six

The Acacia Tree

As I said, my story began in 1953. I was fourteen then. In 1965 I was twenty-six. Those twelve years were full of changes: in three or four years, my entire face changed from a boy's to a man's. During a period of five or six years, Appa died, Amma became a widow; we moved from Mysore to Madhurai,[†] where we lived four years and then we went to Kerala,[†] to Poona,[†] and to Hyderabad.[†] Just as a person goes from self-gratification to real sex, so also there are the many initiations: the first kiss, the first intercourse, the first flight on an airplane, sailing for the first time by steamer on the first foreign trip— all these came to light from hidden sources and from discovering the world of others for the first time.

For many years though, nothing seemed to happen in our lives, as if we were rendered deaf and blind or turned into somnambulants spinning day after day, year after year, like automatons, going home to office to home, from market to home to cinema, from home to bus stand to market to home, from the table to the bed, from the bed to the kitchen, to the bathroom, to the table slowly without our knowledge while growing cataracts in blind eyes and wax in our stuffed ears. The programme that created the entire universe and the original signed versions and the invisible imprint of Amma and Appa on our foreheads all get altered in time, as do our homes, towns, friends, relatives, duties, hairstyles, mustaches, and our love for Kannada and our illusions and fears; all change and from somewhere we find wives, acquire in-laws, beget children, and change from brahmachari[†] to grihastha;[†] and we might as well wonder if such changes in our robotic lives take place due to another indecipherable code—like the transformation of eggs into worms, into the dark-shelled cocoons, and cocoons into butterflies before dying to become another set of eggs—and if our histories and minds have seasons and markers similar to those in plants and trees.

One day in 1953, I was walking with two friends on a street near a college in Mysore. The four o'clock sunshine suddenly changed into a shower, and thousands of golden needles fell on the dusty street. Clouds of dust rose from the heated earth, giving off the intense smell of rain on dry soil. Large drops of rain danced on the tree leaves, turning them shiny and bright.

My two friends and I ran towards the hill near the college. Within two minutes, as we approached the hill breathlessly, the rain stopped suddenly; the sun was shining as if the earth too had been uplifted by that sudden downpour. As we watched, a molten sun emerged from behind the brown clouds—at first as a whirling blue disk, then a bright white wheel, and finally a blinding circle turning the clouds to gold.

I remember the fresh sunshine on Murthy's face lighting up his rich silken hair, as he ran to the student union's toilet, saying, 'I must run.' There was another man with us, but I don't remember his name now. I don't even know which month it was, or which season, but I remember the rain and the sunlit evening, the clouds first, and then the sun, and I do remember my own body was on fire at the exact moment when the raindrops touched the surface of my skin and the surface of the earth, and I remember the leaves and the dusty road.

At the time I did not realize why those moments imprinted themselves in my memory so. I am like that. Revelations occur to me rather gradually. They never strike me like lightning; they do not come to me in the wink of an eye. This is the main difference between me and others like my wife. My revelations are not like roaring waterfalls from cliffs, nor are they quick like electric currents; they are more like slow, slithering tar on a road, like viscous oil, like a slow-moving python.

That evening I was to have my first sexual experience, I think. I understood this much later; I am certain of that. As if plucking the strings of Kama's bow† or as if it were a rainbow or a current of lightning, something went through my body. I must have felt an intense mysterious desire to hug someone immediately. While this memory is now revealing itself, I remember another event, which occurred perhaps the same month.

It happened while I was near the public library and the same kind of sudden rain in brilliant sunshine repeated itself. This time, I was under the yellow-blossomed wattle-laden acacia tree. I was suddenly possessed by an urge to put my arms around the tree, hug it, hug it hard, until its bristling trunk scratched me. For one whole minute I felt transformed, giddy. All the pores of my body swirling like a thousand wheels, I felt drained. When it was over, I was drenched inside and out, slimy wet and damp. A cold wind on my face reminded me that I was sweating. Suddenly I felt ashamed. I looked around to check if anyone had seen my foolish act. I saw a schoolteacher walking on the shining-wet, tarred road holding her black umbrella, carefully lifting the hem of the sari† above her ankles.

I felt guilty and I walked away from that tree. I stood next to a nearby Madana Masti shrub, pretending to sniff its intoxicating flowers. I know now the meaning of Madana Masti—'The Essence of Eros'. Should I change the name of the plant? It appeared to me a fanciful name. Critics may look upon it as a worn-out label, but please note, truth is not only strange, it comes often packaged as a cliché. That Madana Masti was right there.

The schoolteacher held up her sari and kept walking. Her rubber slippers kept spraying mud all around, sounding slop, slop, slop. She walked to the end of the road, turned and disappeared. The next time I went near that tree with Murthy, I could smell the dense fragrance of the shrub, filling the evening air. Murthy was half a year older than I and had a fresh mustache over his lips. Yet, on that intoxicating evening, with the gold of the evening sun and the fragrance of Madana

Masti, he seemed like a pretty girl to me. I felt like hugging him, just as I had hugged the tree earlier. Not sensing my feelings he said, 'Yenamma†—see these Madana Masti flowers? What a great scent.' He plucked a fully open yellow-green flower. I touched its velvety leaves and petals, which felt like a green Champa flower.† Murthy had just learned to address other men teasingly with 'Yenamma', as my brother did. By then, both of us were under the spell of the scent, something resembling the pervasive aroma of ripening mangoes and that of the sugandharaja† flowers in bloom. One yellow-green flower (its leaves were soft as petals to the touch and the flowers were like fruits) I took home, but Amma developed a bad headache from it. I hid the flower in the corner of my desk drawer, along with erasers and pencils, but even as the flower dried and withered over the next three days, its smell filled the room. Amma warned me, 'Be careful when you go near those plants. Their smell attracts snakes—big green snakes which can strike right into the brightness of your eyes.'

Even now I wonder if Murthy also had a similar experience that day. I must ask him the next time I see him. That may have been the reason he ran away to the toilet when it started raining. I clearly remember seeing his smooth tawny cheeks as he handed me the flower and ran off towards the library shouting, 'I must hurry.' That year he also began applying a bit of make-up on his face. He ironed his shirts, started flashing mischievous smiles through his thin mustache. He used his brother's Brylcream for his hair and practised making signs with his fingers to convey naughty messages. At about this time, I started looking at myself in the mirror and began liking my reflection.

As I go over this now, I begin to doubt the veracity of this account. I ask myself whether I am making it all up, whether there was actually a Madana Masti plant in the place, and whether this episode had appeared on the page by association, after reading a vulgar poem sent me by A. K. Ramanujan. I question if it happened just as I told it, and I marvel at whether my first love was indeed a tree, a wattle-laden flowering yellow acacia tree. To the lustful, as they say, there is no fear, no shame. Perhaps first love erupts from the depths, even for a tree, and no matter whether it were embraced by man, woman, or tree, any or all would do. After that, given time, it will learn distinctions. A female tree will know its true mate to be a male tree and not me, K.K. Ramanujan. In my sister's compound in Ahmadabad,[†] they have planted two Natpathi fruit trees, a male and a female. They told me that this was necessary for proper pollination to produce a rich yield of fruit.

I sent what I have written thus far to A. K. Ramanujan. 'It reads like an old story in the *Prajavani*.[†] The Madana Masti descriptions are good,' he said. But I was not sure whether such things should be written in Kannada. In ancient times there were manuals like the *Kama Sutra* and the *Koka Shastra*,[†] both in Sanskrit. But nowadays, in households such as ours, we are more pious; such things are never mentioned.

AKR wrote, 'Go ahead and write. Shed off your frigid inhibition. These days the Kannada poets have started a revolution of sorts in erotic writing. You compared a tree to a lover. Such images are common in Indian and Greek folklore. Remember the Tulsi plant.[†] And see, a tree and a girl are yoked together in a poem I wrote.'

He did send it to me. Take a look:

She, having forgotten
the lamentations of the trunk
in the Koka Shastra,
bristles when kissed,
and showers flowers when kicked.

I ask you, is this a poem?

Chapter Seven

Atthe

1956. I was seventeen, Appa fifty-eight, and Amma forty-eight. That year, for the first time, Appa had a day-long conversation with me. Normally, he didn't speak much; some months he spent his mornings reading the Bhagavadgita.[†] At night he did his office work at home. He went to nearby shops in the evening. Sometimes, he walked as far as Nishadabad.[†] He wouldn't even read the newspaper every day. After he retired, he started getting annoyed with everyone. As his blood pressure increased, so did his hostility towards Amma. Even the sight of her would infuriate him. That year his brother-in-law lay dying with a swollen belly in Madras. Appa had to visit him; I don't know why, but he chose me to go with him to Madras. We caught an express train.

Atthe and her husband lived on a small side street in Georgetown,[†] in an annex near the gate. They had no children. Both husband and wife were obese. Atthe was a short, fair-skinned woman; the parting of her hair showed a four-finger patch of bald scalp where no hair would grow. She took care and applied oil to her hair, combing it till it looked lustrous. Then she would pull her hair back to cover the injured scalp, and double-plaiting, she would twist the braids into a firm bun above the nape of her neck. Her flashing diamond earrings and diamond nose rings on both nostrils were like approaching lights; she was also adorned with a necklace of gold sovereigns, her three-stringed hair ornaments studded with diamonds and rubies, and four gold bangles. On ordinary days most Iyengar women wore ritually washed simple saris, a *mangalsutra*,† and perhaps a gold bangle. But my aging aunt wore, everyday, all her gold and diamonds like a bride. I was somewhat disgusted seeing her bedecked when her husband was lying so ill, with his swollen belly.

'Kuppu!† Kuppu! You've come all the way! You're here!' she said in welcoming my father. 'Ramu! Come, come inside,' she said to me, caressing my head. She took me inside, plucked out a red Madras banana from a bunch hanging from a rope from the ceiling. She peeled it before giving it to me.

'No, no,' I said, hesitating.

'Try it, Ramu; it is very tasty,' she said, coaxing me.

I remembered the long green banana she had given me ten years earlier. Now, this one was red. Perhaps she had not noticed that I was seventeen now. I had seen the red Madras bananas, in the market, but had never tasted one. The inside of the banana had a yellowish-red glow to it. Its dark red peel was thick and had black spots. I took the banana, moved the rind back and forth, and examined it on all sides. It had a reddish hue. It smelled like jackfruit, and like wet earth. When I bit into it, I found that it was not soft. I filled my mouth with its firm flesh, and savoured several more bites. It was a large banana and I wanted to eat all of it, even the six-inch-long strands that hung from it.

My aunt suffered from elephantiasis of the leg. She had a peculiar rhythm to her gait. She dragged her heavy left leg but moved her normal right leg swiftly. Six years ago when she had come to Mysore, I saw her in the backyard one day, sitting near our wash-stone, rubbing her elephant-leg with sesame oil as she held up her sari. Her plump right leg had normal fair skin. The skin on her left leg was deeply wrinkled, with large bead-sized nodules. Her toes were normal, but her left foot was a swollen loaf of bread. Seeing her rub her diseased leg so lovingly, I was disgusted, but felt sorry for her. Sympathy and aversion are close feelings.

I heard Atthe's dhud, dhud, dhadak† elephant-leg gait from behind.

'Ramu, shall I get you some coffee? You liked the banana? Yenappa,[†] eat one more,' she said.

'No, no, I am full,' I said.

'Don't be shy, eat one more. I too like red bananas. They say it is good for my legs; a Malayali[†] doctor told me.'

Emboldened, I looked at her leg and said, 'Is there no cure for this? I thought that in Madras there is a big research hospital!'

'Ayyo! I have been to all those hospitals. It's my karma. In addition to the weight of the heavy leg that I have to lift, once a month I get a high fever for two days. It seems that some sort of worm is living inside this leg. You can't catch it with an operation. At the time of the full moon, each month, the worm in my leg starts to go crazy, and I get fevers. While other people enjoy a full moon and cool moonlit nights, I burn with fever. This worm and I must have been wedded in a past life.'

Atthe's conversation was always spicy. In spite of her illness, her sharp tongue never failed her.

'I suffered in my childhood, and then this for the past ten years. For three months now, he has his belly swollen. With our doctors' bills, we could have raised four children and many grandchildren. This leg of mine is our eldest son, that belly of his is our youngest daughter. I am tired of it,' she said.

My mother told me about Atthe's early years. It's a long story. She was married at ten, fifty years ago, to her husband, the only son of a widow. My aunt's future mother-in-law was a strange woman, to say the least. Even though she was an Iyengar, she worshiped in the Kali temple[†] and she knew black magic. Amma said, her talk was as smooth as pulling a strand of hair out of butter or, as Atthe herself would have said, 'as smooth as a needle through a banana', but she was a hardened calcified type. Being a controlling woman, she didn't like it when her son, at sixteen, began roaming around with a Madras drama company, and started coming home late at night. To get her son on a proper track, she devised a plan. When no one was around, she went to my grandfather's house three streets from the Parthasarathi Temple.[†]

She told him, 'Acharya,[†] my house is barren without a married woman. How long will I live like this? I have a house in the village. There are three acres from my late husband. And jewellery too. My son is now sixteen; your daughter is already ten and as pretty as the Goddess Laxmi.[†] Give her to my son in marriage. That would be a boon. As for the wedding expenses, spend only as much as you can afford.'

That was clever of her. My grandfather lacked business acumen. He had seen this poor widow's handsome son who wore peanut-sized earrings. Grandfather did not hesitate. He agreed on the alliance. Back at the house, my grandmother was very worried and agitated. That widow's treachery, black magic, and sorcery were well known in the entire town, and she was going to be her daughter's mother-in-law—what a fate! That night, with great hesitation, grandmother went to her husband and said,

'Don't you know about that old woman? They say she is cruel, treacherous, well versed in black magic. They say even going near her would be dangerous.'

'Where did you go and hear all that? You should have stayed home,' he said.

'Don't get mad. Listen to me. You have your daughter's entire future in your hands. Having raised her as a parrot, now you are willing to sacrifice her to a wild cat! Better push her off into a well,' grandmother said.

'Where did you learn to speak like this? You were meek all these days, suddenly you have grown a new tongue,' he said, glaring at his wife.

Grandfather was short-tempered. Often he beat his own wife. He was jealous and suspicious. He forbade his wife to step outside the house. One day when she went to the temple, she wore a bit more flowers than usual. That evening at the auspicious hour at dusk, he beat her up, shouting, 'Wearing so many flowers like a whore! Who is your lover?' His staring eyes were red and furious. He shredded the petals off the *kanakambra*† flower set aside for prayers, and threw them into the front yard. That was the kind of Brahmin he was. Scared and distraught, grandmother rolled her eyes and lamented, 'My god, such improper words! At such an auspicious hour! This house is doomed.' She prayed touching her mangalsutra.†

The same night he made up his mind about his daughter's wedding, my grandfather warned my grandmother once again. He said, 'Keep your mouth shut now. I am the man in this house. My promise to that woman is final.' I never met him or grandmother. We didn't even have their photograph in our house. Grandfather died the year of my birth and grandmother died three years later.

Those events must have taken place in 1906 or 1907. Many, many years later, Atthe told the story to Amma, who then told it to me. The first time I heard it, I felt like an old man of fifty, as if I had witnessed Atthe's life with my own eyes and ears. I could see them in the light of the kerosene lamp in the bedroom of their house in Thiruvellikkeni;† I could see my middle-aged grandfather, and grandmother, ten years younger than he, standing small in front of him. She was scared and in pain. He was shouting in a rage, and it being night, his shining forehead had no *namam*† on it. I felt I was present and could see him walking off towards the front bathroom, shaking his towel.

Atthe, my Chikkatthe,† was married off when she was ten. At eleven she started having her periods, and the marriage was consummated. Her husband was seventeen then, hot and raw; she was eleven, tender and innocent. I wondered what he inflicted on her in bed the first night and what she had to undergo, and I wondered if such violent initiations were ever mended. But, whether healed or not, their marriage survived, in anger and love, and ripened into old age.

Atthe entered her in-law's house at age eleven. Little did she know that she was entering hell. The mother-in-law couldn't tolerate the young couple's intimacy. The husband and wife were made to sleep in the next room; they had to listen to the moans and groans of the mother who couldn't sleep. Even through their hurried love-making, Atthe would have to worry about her mother-in-law next door. The mother-in-law herself was worried that with her son's marriage, her own power in the house would dwindle. 'I found a slut for my son. Witch! She is brainwashing him with magic potions,' she grumbled, spreading rumours around town. She mocked and teased her daughter-in-law. She pinched her, pushed her around, and only permitted her to eat after everyone else had eaten. She had to eat from the same plate which her husband had used. Her mother-in-law didn't allow her to put any oil on her hair. Pretending to help comb her hair, she pulled Atthe's hair. Day and night she nagged her daughter-in-law. Her son loved his wife; he was young and interested in their physical intimacy. At night he secretly gave his wife bananas to eat; he gave her cardamom-laced betel leaves[†] and areca nuts to chew; he came home to eat and went to bed early.

The voodoo the mother-in-law practised boomeranged, her schemes backfired, and she could not stand the changes in her son. She felt that the thorns had turned up in her own plate of rice. Still, she continued plotting to keep her son and his wife apart.

Amma said, 'She caused them many hardships, not just one or two. She mixed gravel in the rice secretly, and asked her daughter-in-law to serve her son. He ate it and yelled at his wife. Once she bought four tiny needles from a gypsy woman, hid them in a pile of rice pilaf. Your Atthe somehow found out and removed the needles before serving her husband. Yet, she was scared that her mother-in-law might still have poisoned his meal. The old woman was hoping that her son would find those needles in his rice and become enraged. But it didn't happen. When her plan failed, she became even more spiteful. For the moment, your Atthe and her husband were out of harm's way.'

One day, six months later, the old woman gave her daughter-in-law a bottle of bath oil and said, 'His eyes are red and his body has excess heat. Give him a good, cleansing warm oil bath.'

So Atthe helped her husband get ready for the oil bath. She made him sit in his white underwear on the stone slab in the bathroom. She mixed hot and cold water to the proper warmth. She applied the oil carefully on his well-built shining dark body; on his crown, on the sides of his head, his eyebrows and ears, and around his neck; she rubbed and dabbed that oil with all her devotion and tenderness. But, within five minutes she felt something was wrong. Her husband's head and body began burning wherever the oil had been applied. His eyes became red. How could she have suspected such treachery from his own mother? The old woman had mixed chili powder in the bath oil, boiled the concoction, strained it off to remove traces of peppers, cooled the oil again, and had given it to her daughter-in-law for use on her husband. His body was on fire. As his head, eyes, ears and nose began burning, he shouted, 'You bitch. Slut! Burning me with your witchcraft! Let me give you a dose of what's coming to you!'

From the bathroom stove, he picked up a piece of burning wood, slammed it on the thirteen-year-old's head. She bled. He dragged her. Pulling her with all his force, he dumped her out of the front door on to the street.

His mother acted as if she had no clue about what was happening. She came out and said,

'What's the matter, Rangu! Can't you wear at least a loin-cloth?' Then she ran back to the bathroom, brought out the bath oil bottle, and pretending to examine it, shouted, 'See, how red this oil is! She has added something horrible to it—the she-devil!' She ran out, pulled the blood-drenched hair off her daughter-in-law's head, slammed her on the ground and kicked her. She threw mud and stone pebbles at her, yelling, 'Let someone set a torch to your face; let your womb be seared with red coal!'

Atthe shielded her face and body, and ran to her mother's house. Her Amma, my grandmother, was shocked to see her daughter at ten in the morning in such a state. She took her in and bolted the door. Sobbing, she washed her daughter's wounds in the bathroom, cleaned her face with warm water, wiped the face dry, and placed kumkum[†] on her forehead. Just then they heard a banging on the door. Atthe begged, crying out, 'Please don't open the door…don't. They will kill me!' So the door remained shut. Atthe's mother-in-law was screaming, 'You filthy rotten devil! What a degenerate stock you come from! Slut! Open the door. I shall call the police! Nobody slams the door on me. Believe me, I shall uproot this house! Let me speak to the man of the house—he is the one with whom I arranged this marriage! I know your vile deceptions. But you don't know what power I have! I will turn this house upside down. You will see.'

For fifteen minutes she stayed there shouting imprecations at them. Then she walked back to her home, three streets away, mouthing her poisonous slander for the benefit of listeners at their windows.

Atthe cried all that day, her face becoming swollen; her mother tried to console her, but to no avail. Later Atthe told Amma about what happened.

'Most people lose bladder control when they get scared, but even though I ran to the bathroom ten times that day, not a drop would come out. But at night, I had no more control than an infant; I wet myself, drenching my sari. I felt disgust at the smell of my own urine. That was my fate!'

After Atthe left her mother-in-law's house, she did not return there for twelve years. Grandmother, who was usually helpless in all other matters, could not let this injustice continue. She insisted that her husband not send their daughter back to her in-laws. Grandfather was upset and angry too. He disagreed initially, but over time he realized reluctantly the mistake he had made; he pitied his daughter, and was pained to see her suffer so much. When the mother-in-law came back to see him, he did not speak to her. She argued, she yelled abuses at them, she threatened a lawsuit. He rebuked her in silence. Taking his lead, others also stopped talking to the old woman. Not once did anyone exchange a word with her. No matter how often she came, they acted as if no one had come. To them she had ceased to exist; they stared through her, as if nobody was there and nothing had happened.

They would go about their everyday routines. Her shrieks and imprecations lost power in the face of their unseeing eyes and deaf ears. Then she sent her son. When he came, they made sure that Atthe was sent to the kitchen, securely locked inside. He too was met with the same stony silence. The parents swallowed their pride and did not respond; they blotted out the pleading and shouting.

The old woman then threatened that she would get her son married again. That didn't work. Somehow, she even managed to poison grandfather with one of her evil potions. He lost his appetite and his sleep; he became dull and listless. He took off from his PWD office work for weeks. They arranged special prayers for him in the temple. Grandmother took him to a sorcerer in the Nungumbakkum graveyard,[†] a red-eyed magician wearing kumkum and a turmeric-dyed loincloth who blessed grandfather with the *hraam hreem* mantra[†] and touched his head with a broom made of neem[†] leaves. He gave grandfather a concoction of coconut water, fresh mother's milk, and kumkum powder to drink. Grandfather vomited a rupee-sized black slimy object and then he was cured.

After this, there was no talk of sending the daughter to the in-law's house. Fortunately for Atthe, as long as the mother-in-law lived, everyone stayed away from her. It is said that the old woman even tried poisoning her own son by using one of her evil potions. Amma said, 'Such people keep up their practice. When they don't find a victim they don't even mind poisoning their own brothers, sisters, sons, or husbands. The evil spirit in them forces them to do such things.'

Her son, my uncle, ran away with the drama troop and roamed around from town to town. His mother became more insane. She went about shouting abuses not only at her daughter-in-law and my grandparents, but at anyone and everyone in town. She wore dirty rags and didn't even bathe regularly. When the landlord went to collect rent, he found her unconscious in the bathroom and carried her to the hall. Her kitchen had not been cleaned for weeks. Pots and pans were scattered all over. Someone tried to find the whereabouts of her son's drama company. A message finally reached him; he rode a bus home from Salem to Madras. By then her body had begun to rot.

'What a life!' Amma said. 'Look at your aunt's forehead the next time you see her. The scar at the parting of her hair is still there.'

I looked for that scar and found it. There it was, as evidence. Proof of the old story, right at the parting of her hair. I observed the patch of thick, wrinkled skin where not a single hair grew.

Now I see this same aunt, wearing a three-diamond nose-ring, and ten-diamond earrings. Amma told me that Atthe had a jewel box in her cupboard filled with more such diamonds, jewellery, rings, armbands, wristbands, and bracelets.

Her husband continued to be a vagabond for twelve more years after his mother's death. Then he returned to Madras, found a job as a clerk in a post office and decided to settle down. His postcard announced abruptly that he had found a job, rented a house in Georgetown, and would come on such and such a day for their daughter.

One Friday he came in a rented, horse-drawn cart which waited outside. He swallowed coffee in a single gulp and took home his wife who was waiting for him. They called him 'Attimbeeru'. She wore a simple sari, and carried a suitcase as if it contained her entire life. My grandparents were stunned. They said little. Their daughter was now twenty-five. Grandfather was worn out complaining, and grandmother was tired of listening to his complaints. Their daughter was fed up with everything. Atthe had found her situation intolerable, for had not grandmother seen her daughter standing near the well at the back of the annex and had she not run out and saved her daughter from the well and taken her indoors and hugged and kissed her? After that grandmother had never allowed Atthe to go anywhere near the well to fetch water.

None of them knew what to expect, but at least for the time being, Atthe's wish to join her husband was fulfilled. Her husband wore earrings. He took off his tuft of hair and wore a neat haircut. At thirty he had started graying already, but he had been pious and austere;

he offered twilight prayers each day. He drew closer to his wife. He sang old love songs from his drama roles. There was new laughter and gaiety in the house.

By now Atthe also had matured. Having lived for twelve years with grandmother, she was now an expert cook. She, besides making the traditional *saru*,[†] made *sambar*,[†] *pulkiyogare*[†] sour rice; she also made *pheni*,[†] *chiroti*[†] and other desserts better than anyone else. Her conversation had sharpened too. She had zest; she was quick-witted and had an ironic voice. She controlled her husband with food and the charm of her talk. She saved money. With a clever instalment plan she purchased a new piece of jewellery each year. She became known for her beautiful Mysore silk, Kanchipuram, and Kollegala saris;[†] her skill in getting the best prices when shopping, her amusing wedding songs, and her laughter.

Attimbeeru had mellowed and was under his wife's control now. He also loved other people's children. When he came to Mysore once, he thrilled us by reciting a court jester's poem from Raja Veera Simha, a Tamil version of *King Lear* by Sambandam Modeleyar. That was the first time I heard the *King Lear* story; I must have been eight or nine then. Ten years later, when I read Shakespeare in college, I had forgotten my uncle's version of *King Lear*, but Raja Veera Simha's vague descriptions ran alongside the Shakespeare text, like a blurry face seen from a train window. One day in my junior BA class, as I dozed off I dreamt of Attimbeeru sitting in our upstairs bedroom with me, my neighbour Raja, and my brothers and sisters. There he was, with his huge body and a soft voice, chewing tobacco and areca nut with betel leaves, telling stories from high drama. This dream ended with a replay of Attimbeeru's version of the Lear story.

Attimbeeru knew another art. Once when he visited us for three days, he staged a show of finger shadows for us children. He moved the table lamp near the door. He sat in front of it, stretched his hands with a handkerchief hanging from one finger, and he created all sorts of animal images on the wall. In one half-hour, we saw a barking dog with its ears raised and teeth gnawing, running at us to bite; a male dog on top of a female dog performing a vulgar act; a sailing duck with a white hole for an eye chasing to catch a fish with its beak; the same duck then would be stretching its back and its long neck, and using its beak to groom its feathers; or there would be a turban-wearing man walking in haste and then slipping on a banana peel to fall flat on the road.

We were immersed in a world of shadows, watching our uncle. After thirty minutes he said, 'The show is over, my friends! Turn on the lights and take this table lamp to your father's room.' Only then did we come back to earth. I remember Attimbeeru's shining, silver hair, his dark, educated face and white teeth, his earrings with yellow gemstones, and his clever long dark fingers stretching from the sleeves of his Nehru shirt.[†]

That was the last of his shadow shows. The next day he gave one more private show for Raji and me since we were the youngest. He taught us how to create the shadow of a snarling dog with teeth exposed. I have put on this show many times since then. Once when I was at a party in America, where I first met my future wife Joanie, I performed a show for her. I went to a corner, removed the shade from the table lamp, and performed what Attimbeeru had taught me. I made my shadowplay dog bite the shadow of Joanie's nose, and then I kissed her and romanced her. Within one week, instead of my shadowplay dog biting her nose, it was I who was kissing her in a bathtub. I even bit her nose softly, wiping off soap bubbles and tasting its tangy taste. See, what leads to what.

Now, the same Attimbeeru was lying in bed with a blown-up belly. A rubber tube ran from his abdomen. A white-uniformed nurse placed the end of that tube in a side bucket, pumping the liquid. The tube was semi-transparent. His body fluids moved noisily up and down through the tube. His unshaven, dark face appeared like the head of a knotted silver stick; he had on the same earrings but there were no smiles. His face sagged as if he had swallowed his pain. His silent eyes were shut. They gave him medicines, orange juice, and glucose water, using the same conch shell through which he used to give us castor oil when we were children. If he asked for anything else, Atthe would order him, 'Don't ask for the same thing a hundred times like a baby. Just sleep quietly. In an hour I will give you one more dose of glucose water.'

Turning to us she said, 'All night long he fussed. Had no sleep for three weeks. I'll run a fever from his nonsense.' She stretched her swollen elephant-leg and sighed. Right at that moment her husband looked at her, like a little calf begging its mother for something. Appa said to him, 'Don't tire yourself. I will go see your doctor and get an update.'

Appa gave his sister the bag of oranges we had brought and some ten-rupee notes saying, 'Be back tomorrow. I have to see my lawyer. You know about Alamelu.' Alamelu was my great-aunt, the eldest sister of my father. Her own story is another long Ramayana.

'Of course, we know about Alamelu. Only you can do something about it. But both of you can stay here if you like,' Atthe said.

'No, why do you need to bother to cook for us? I will not be of much help to you anyway. Come along, Ramu. Let's go.' When we got out, Appa said, 'The toilets in Georgetown make me want to throw-up.'

Chapter Eight

Home

These stories might have been better served by Tamil, the language in which Amma told me all about Atthe. In my early years, I spoke Madras Tamil to Amma, in the kitchen of our Mysore home; I switched to Mysore Tamil with our Iyengar housemaids who cooked; outside the house, I spoke Kannada with my friends. Upstairs in his office Appa conversed in English with his friends and with my brother. By 1956, I too spoke English upstairs when I went to Appa's study. Thus, upstairs–downstairs, inside–outside, I grew accustomed to three languages. Coming down from father's study, I translated to myself, and now that I am in this country, my troubles and my thoughts seem to need a translator again. I write, think, love, and dream sometimes in Kannada, sometimes in Tamil. This synchrony existed in the written more than in the spoken language. Father's study upstairs contained a desk with a green felt pad, books in English and in Sanskrit, and a radio to one side. On the walls there were photographs of the snow-capped Alps and of the Himalayas, a picture of the Queen Mary steamer, and even a picture of the Queen of England. There were many calendars on the wall and several group photographs from Appa's time. On the desk were a stack of files and a cash box. Appa controlled all household expenses from his office upstairs. He even had an electric calling bell to summon Amma or me. When he wanted coffee to be brought up, it had to be served in china. Upstairs, in his office, he would drink coffee slowly, sipping from the edges of the cup. Downstairs, according to custom, he would pour the drink from a silver cup into his mouth, without contact to his lips.

Amma's domain was downstairs. She ruled over her children, housemaids, and even the occasional helper hired for cooking. We slept in the great hall or rooms located downstairs. When he had a cold or fever, Appa too stayed away from upstairs. Downstairs, Amma's embroidery and a large photograph of Appa and smaller ones of the children and relatives were framed and hung on the walls.

The back entrance to our house was for the vendors of curds, vegetables, and peanuts. It was also the customary entrance for the man hired to pluck coconuts, or for the barber who made his fortnightly visit bringing Appa hot gossip from the palace. In those days, even payments in small change would have to come from upstairs from the cash box in Appa's study.

In the front yard we grew jasmine, the sugandha flower, and a decorative English patch with yellow or red-speckled crotons and three kinds of roses. In the backyard Amma grew eggplants, green beans, string beans, and okra. There were coconut trees, tulsi plants, stone slabs for washing clothes, storage areas for firewood and coal, and shaded by the spreading branches of a giant sampige[†] tree nearby, a roofless outdoor toilet that was open to bird droppings and raindrops.

We used two kinds of stairs to get to the second floor. The stairs in the front were strong, made of solid wood; at the back there was a shaky stepladder in use, which was less secure. Different classes of people entered from the front or the back of the house. The front was meant for Appa, his friends, and later, my grown-up brother Gopi. I used the back entrance, as did the occasional hired help. The ladder took us to the attic where we dried our clothes on lines strung between bamboo poles. Once Amma gave shelter in that attic to a poor friend of hers whose husband had thrown her out. The woman slept right under one bamboo pole. Sometimes, when water dripped off the line, the woman sat in a corner of the attic.

That is how we lived: front and back, upstairs and downstairs, reflecting the social order, making it a model house for our Marxist critics.

From the balcony on the second floor, with another stepladder, we could get on to the roof, and see our neighbours' tiled roofs, the palace, and the Clock Tower. To one side lay the bright blue Chamundi Hill, like a ceremonial elephant half-asleep, sometimes cloud-mantled. At night we saw the hill illuminated with rows of bright lights. During Navaratri festival, the hilltop temple, the palace (which was later converted into a hotel), and the main palace near the market were all illuminated. Exactly at seven in the evening, someone would turn on a switch, lighting up millions of bulbs outlining palaces and temples. On such nights it looked as if someone must have turned off the stars over the Mysore sky.

We could see none of these at ground level, or from father's office upstairs. From our windows downstairs and in our backyard we could see a glowing sky, but for a view of the entire sky, the palace, and the hill, we had to get up to the roof.

Chapter Nine

The Rickshaw Man

I don't remember going back again to Atthe's Georgetown house. We were out in the sweltering heat of Madras. Appa hired a rickshaw to take us to his niece's house in Purasavaakkam.[†]

I had seen rickshaws before, but never rode in one. The rickshaw puller, the human machine, grinned at us. He flattened his lips between pointer and middle finger and ejected a trajectory of red betel juice, shooting it sure as an arrow and on to the pavement. We climbed into the rickshaw. He lifted its handles, connected straps to the wheels, turned his back to us and began running, dragging the rickshaw. The sudden jerk jolted us back. 'Mindless rascal,' Appa cursed under his breath. I kept glancing at the driver's back, his long neck, his oil-slicked, shining black hair, his black headband that caught some of the sweat that began to pour down in the blazing heat of Madras. Appa, a fat man of 170 pounds, sat in style. Even on a hot day, he had on his formal wear: a shirt and a jacket over his Finley dhoti,[†] a long scarf around his neck, and a colourful turban on his head. He wore his *shree churna*, the long vertical red line on the forehead. I saw sweat dripping in rivulets down the driver's black back, and watched his strong muscles rippling. For the first time in my life I wondered if it was proper for a man to be turned into a machine, or for a man to be turned into a draught animal pulling people. Appa, dabbing his face with his scarf, said to me, 'One should be careful with these fellows. They are rogues, every one of them! If you are new to the city, they will drag you on a joyride and charge you three rupees.' Having said that, Appa realized that he had not settled the fare.

'Listen, you rickshawman! You have to take us to the fourth house in Ramaswami Modeleyar Road in Purasavaakkam—how much do you charge?'

The man replied in his rickshawman's Tamil, 'Sir, you know, just give me what you think is right. I shall accept it as a gift. Lighter than a feather, you and the young master will be flying there. Judge for yourself.'

Taken aback at such slippery doubletalk Appa said, 'Ho! Ho! Stop! You better settle the fare right now. I'll give you one rupee.'

'Sir, see for yourself how comfortable your ride will be and then decide what to pay me. Why worry now?'

'I know you'll demand more money afterwards. You rickshaw pullers are all the same. Better settle the fare now or else stop the rickshaw right here. We'll get off.'

His words were of no use. The rickshaw man increased his speed, and kept running, dragging the rickshaw at a slick pace. His back was now thoroughly drenched with sweat. I felt sorry for him. I am putting down what I remember. The sight of huge buildings on either side; the bicycles, the cars, other rickshaws; a bridge, a river, the smell of urinals; the sight of men defecating along the beach, people cleansing themselves with buckets of water, laundrymen washing white uniforms (perhaps linen from the nearby hospital). All these kept me engrossed and I forgot the human engine dragging us.

As we made a turn on to another street, I saw a huge Sikh† man, standing near a municipal tap wearing only a narrow loincloth. He removed his turban and placed it aside. He was applying bath oil over his hairy body in deliberate slow strokes. The hair from his head flowed down his back, and he had a long beard on his unshaven face. He placed his palms on his jaw, turned his neck in slow exercise motion while stretching himself upwards. Usually the place would be filled with women—quarrelling gossiping women. They would have been there with bronze pots and buckets to fetch water. The women would have been chattering and huddling in droves around the jetting phallic municipal taps. It being early afternoon, no women were in sight. The Sikh had the place to himself. He stood there, with his eyes shut, seeming to meditate. I could see that he was deeply engaged in the sensuous pleasure of massaging his own body with bath oil.

I had spotted him clearly from about a furlong away, as if I were looking through well-focused binoculars, and as we approached the municipal tap, like a movie camera closing in from a long shot, I began to see more details. Each strand of hair was distinctly visible. I felt like getting down from the rickshaw to see him closer with a magnifying lens. There was no need for it though, as my internal camera was already very close, peering at him. I could see a fistful of pubic hair escaping from the sides of his G-string, revealing the bulge of his cardamom-coloured banana-sized crotch. He must have oiled it too. Even after our rickshaw passed, I kept turning back to stare at this self-stroking man. As our rickshaw made its turn, I saw the man turn on the tap; he bent down and placed first his buttocks, then his back, and then his entire body under the tap to wash himself.

When I came to my senses again, my eyes were on the rickshawman in front of me pulling the rickshaw, and his sweat-drenched muscular back. I felt guilty. I had been so mesmerized by the sight of the Sikh, but now I turned my attention to watching rows of hutments, kids with drippy noses, bare-breasted slum women removing lice from each other's long hair.

Finally we reached Purasavaakkam. Appa and the rickshawman started to argue about the fare.

'At the least, three rupees, sir! I have carried you five miles, thinning my blood!' the driver spat out angrily. Then he added softly, 'Consider my stomach, lord!'

I saw his stomach. Dark, shining, emaciated. Like the rest of us, he too had a navel. But unlike some with huge, rupee-sized, bulging protrusions, his was just a tiny slit, like the navels of fashionably thin film stars in American movies. Probably he was born in a desolate slum, with no doctor or midwife to help. It could be that a neighbour woman dragged him out of his mother's womb, severed the umbilical cord with her mouth, breaking him from the mother's bond. Now, here was the fully grown son, standing in front of us, arguing for an extra rupee. (I am not sure if I thought all these then, or I am colouring what I saw.)

'Right, right! Just leave off. Take this!' Appa said, and he gave him one-and-a-half rupees in a seemingly magnanimous gesture.

'Sir! Sir! Please don't hurt my stomach! I have three children,' he said.

The human machine had now turned into a beggar.

'Fine, fine. Get lost! I told you at the start, not to bargain with us later.'

Then Appa turned to me and said, 'Come along. Let's go.' He led the way into the house.

The rickshaw driver removed his black headband, wiped his sweat and grumbled in Tamil. Having made sure that Appa had gone inside, I took out a half-rupee coin from my pocket and gave it to the man. He said, 'Sir, I am a poor man; you have a great heart. Ah, there is a god, to be sure!' He saluted me. I was glad that the man who had quarrelled with Appa was now praising me.

But later, when they told me that nobody paid more than a rupee for a rickshaw to cover that distance, I felt stupid. The next day I saw the same rickshaw driver near Moor Market chatting with friends. He was holding a fully peeled banana in his hand. As I watched, he placed the banana in his mouth and moved it in and out. His eyes were on a nearby eunuch with a flat chest, decked out in bracelets, a red blouse, and a dirty green outfit; he was clean-shaven, but had a full head of woman's hair. He stared back at the driver and kept chewing his betel leaves. The rickshaw puller said, 'Yené, how about in that gully there? I'll give two annas,'† and repeated his vulgar banana gesture. The eunuch swayed his hips coyly, replied in his sly cajoling yet masculine voice, 'For two annas? Do you take me for a cheap whore?' That is when the driver caught sight of me. He hid the banana quickly. Smiling broadly, he said, 'Do you need a ride today too, sir?' First I pretended not to have seen him, but then I said 'No, no,' and, as I walked away briskly, I noticed a large tattoo on the driver's forearm that I had not noticed the day before.

Later that day, as we waited for hours to find a table for two in Ananda Bhavan restaurant to eat some crisp masala vada,[†] I forgot all about the afternoon.

Chapter Ten

On Latrines

Now, twenty years later, 10,000 miles away, I remember many things I did not think I would. It's like the Madras beach, where the more you dig in the sand, the more water you will find. Once a doctor told me, though we defecate every day, fecal matter from twenty years ago might still be lining our twenty-two feet of small intestine and six feet of large intestine. It must be like karma, twenty years of arrears sticking to us. My wife too heard this from the doctor. Whenever I brought up old stuff, she would say, 'Like that doctor said—that's crap from twenty years ago!'

Thinking of that, I remember Appa saying, 'I hate the lavatory in Atthe's Georgetown house. It disgusts me.' But I couldn't tell why he thought the latrine in the Purasavaakkam house would be less horrible. As you entered the front door, you took ten steps into a shallow passageway lighted with only a dim yellow bulb, and there at the end of the gully facing you was the latrine with the tin door and latch. Inside, you found a cement floor with the raised imprint of two feet and, between them, the wide hole. Underneath, at a lower level, you would see the bucket with the day's dung; some droppings would have missed the mark, and there would be the buzz of bluebottle flies flitting about below. No need to describe all this; everyone remembers no doubt.

I had a new toilet experience on my visit to Madras. Beyond the bucket of dung, there was a small rusted backdoor. When I was in there, squatting on the raised footpads and poised over the hole, the backdoor opened without warning and a hand stretched in from somewhere. It pulled the bucket back, quickly emptying it outside and replacing the emptied bucket in its original place, releasing once again the same fetid smell as before. I was horribly disgusted.

That afternoon on Third Street, I saw a stinking municipal truck. A man was carefully emptying buckets into larger containers. The entire street smelled of human excrement. As the truck started moving to the next street, the man got on it and, like an army commander, held his outstretched arm away from his body, staring at the sky. A sweeper woman stood on the corner, holding a pouch for supari[†] in one hand and a fan-shaped broom tucked under her arm. She was dabbing lime on betel leaves. She was pregnant. I was not sure whether it was a woman's or man's hand snatching the bucket from below me; it could well have been the hand of a pregnant woman. I felt disgusted. My skin crawled with embarrassment as I looked at her.

As these details are coming to me now, it occurs to me that this woman and her entire clan came to know us only through our excrement. Theirs was an upside-down view of the world. Just because it was their lot, something they did to earn their keep, was it any the less disgusting to them? And wouldn't they, who are condemned to such an existence, be enraged eventually?

I saw her, chewing her pan, and she seemed patient and calm. Would her unborn child have remained as calm and patient? Thinking of this, I felt scared as I considered the matter twenty years later. If all had gone well for them, her son, now twenty, could very well be studying in a college or he could be active in politics or he might be a clerk or, worst of all, he could be cleaning toilets.

In the old days, except for royalty who had proper toilets, all others went into the fields, as is done even now in villages. No one handled another man's nightsoil. Like they say, 'The water in the pond must get back to the pond.' Our method of recycling was automatic: food into manure and manure into food.

My wife Joanie often tells me that the Western invention of the modern toilet was not a simple contraption, but an instrument of social revolution. I didn't tell you about this in the right order. In 1960 when I was in Bangalore, Joanie worked in Cochin as a Peace Corps volunteer from America. (Note: AKR translated the word 'volunteer' into Kannada for me.) Neither she nor I ever dreamed that she and I would meet and get married. In Cochin she had seen such municipal nightsoil trucks. She heard all about the disposal of human excrement there. It seems that they dumped the entire city's excreta into septic tanks, which would then be treated with chemicals to be deodorized and sanitized, thus transforming human waste into manure. The municipalities were always in need of special kinds of workers willing to work on human excreta. The pollution and the poisonous fumes from the sewage treatment tanks would be so great that the workers' lives were shortened by such exposure. Strangely though, even for such a life-threatening labour, there were long lines of applicants. The competition was high. Many had to bribe officials, or get patronage chits. That kind of work would pay 200 rupees a month, as compared to just fifty rupees a month for other municipal cleaning jobs. For twenty years I have known all this, and yet like others, I too have been leading a life unconcerned about any of it.

Each time I used a latrine in Madras, I was afraid of another hand sticking in from the trapdoor to grab the bucket. I was afraid that my dung might fall on those hands, or worse, someone might try to take a look through that door.... The next day there was an unusual sound near the toilet; I heard a gnawing sound at the back door, and then a light-pink snout appeared, and I saw a piglet with a curly tail running in, right below me. I can't tell you how scared I was! I said, 'Shoo! Shoo!' throwing water at it with the dipper. I washed myself quickly and ran out sweating.

Though I have used similar latrines a few times in Dharwar, Belgaum,[†] Kerala and Poona, my early terror of using such latrines has never subsided. Some places used disposable baskets made of palm tree leaves. About a year later, when I first went to Bombay, I saw a modern toilet in a rich man's house. The entire house had ceramic tiles. Even the toilet bowl was bright white ceramic china. I was afraid of using such a neat toilet. Like a naïve villager, I kept admiring the shining piece of whiteness. Now they are so common we take them for granted.

I sent the above pages to AKR. I was embarrassed at having written such stuff; after all, once it is printed even respectable women and children might read the book. I also worried that they might see these concerns of mine as bourgeois thoughts and ascribe them to my American wife's influence.

Or they might say, 'You have gone a bit too far this time, but don't worry. Even "disgust", *bibhatsa*[†] in Sanskrit, is one of the nine muses. Some critics may tear you apart, but let it be.'

Or, they might say, 'If a trip from Mysore to Madras made you write like this, think of those who have been abroad. For them what you've written would be quite familiar! They always see such things very clearly. You know about Naipaul. In Calcutta, even Gandhi cleaned toilets to make his point.'

I am not sure whether AKR was in town. It is possible he didn't like what I sent him. He had no comments on this part of my writing. When he sent my manuscript back, he had put down the word, 'defecation'.

Thank goodness, he did not include a poem.

When I think of those memories now, I agree, that for someone like me who had never left Mysore, Madras was another country. Though I had hardly gone 300 miles, it felt foreign to me.

Chapter Eleven

The Naming of Names

That night we stayed in Amrutha's house in Purasavaakkam. Doddappa had two daughters: Amrutha and Vasundhara. I addressed these two, my cousins, as Amruthamami, and Vasundharamami. Vasundhara had lost her husband when she was very young and had been living with Amrutha since then. (At the time, there was also a plump Tamil film star with the name Vasundhara.) Unlike Amrutha, Vasundhara was dark; she was just under five feet, and being a widow, she wore no kumkum or jewellery. Yet, she had a charming face. Amrutha had two daughters, six and seven years old—one fair, and the other darker like Vasundhara. This gave the whole household a sort of symmetry, a balancing contrast.

Amrutha's eldest son was fifteen. He was younger than I was; he was also named Ramanuja. Among Iyengars in Madras there were many with that name. They called him Ramu too. But when I saw him, and heard them calling him Ramu, I felt a bit strange. Sometimes when they called him I would reply. Soon, they nicknamed me 'Mysore Ramu'. He was thin, tall, and bony. He wore the three red marks of the Iyengar namam on his forehead; I have never worn a namam. Although we shared a common name, he was born somewhere else, grew up differently, had sisters, and his fate was different from mine. A few years earlier in a different relative's house, I had met another boy named Ramanuja. He was related to me through Amma and his father was a chief engineer. I played cricket with him in an alley by his house in Mambalam.[†] There was talk that his sister Kamu might get married to my brother. Even my mother hoped for this connection, and my brother too found the suggestion agreeable. But Appa consulted Atthe, who prepared two long lists of specific demands. One asked for earrings, a nose-ring with five gemstones, a gold-laced belt weighing a pound, bracelets, eight bangles, a wedding ring with red and white diamonds, and items for the groom. Her list gave the details of the weights and the carats for the diamonds, their costs, and the Chettiyar shop[†] from where to buy them. In her second list, she specified silver utensils, plates, pots and pans; shirts and suits for the groom, and the like. She gave the lists to Appa, and advising him, said, 'To match your family status and that of theirs, ask them to get at least the items on the two lists. Only then give consent.'

On his own Appa would not have wanted any of it. But as Amma explained it later, his nature was such that he could get tempted. Shamelessly, he gave the lists to the chief engineer, whose face sagged on seeing the demands. The prospect of an alliance was never mentioned again. Kamu was well proportioned, fair-skinned and pretty. My mother liked her too. With the talk of marriage in the air, Kamu had assumed a dignified demeanour. I was fifteen then; I too began liking that face of hidden smiles, her thick long hair and the lemon-sized bulges beneath her white blouse. We never saw that family again.

I told you about another Ramanuja, Kamu's brother, in that house. I saw his photograph ten years later in The Hindu[†] newspaper. He was modelling in a Kolyinos Toothpaste[†] ad. In it I saw his young, handsome face with pearly-white teeth. Like his father he became an engineer. He had grown up among affluent young men in Madras, and he became well known because of the advertisement. Two years later, in 1965, when I went back to India, my Srirangam[†] uncle said, 'Do you know about that Mambala Ramanuja? He got married to the daughter of a very rich man who owned a huge pharmaceutical company. I was at his wedding. Within a month of the wedding he went away for a conference in Germany, bidding goodbye to his wife at the Delhi airport. His plane crashed on the Alps in a heavy snowstorm, falling into the valley bellow, killing all seventy-one passengers. Not a single one survived. Not even a body part could be found. He had the same name as yours, Ramanuja,' suggesting as if he was wondering whether that Ramanujan had died instead of me.

My brother finally got married in 1960. The name of his new bride was also Kamu. Things no doubt recur due to old unfulfilled desires or from subconscious longings to find a girl with the same name as the one before. Do people sharing identical names belong to identical sects? Other than the name, they may have little in common. Does membership by birth and the mantra of shared names, give anyone a deeper affinity?

Chapter Twelve

Narcissus Sees His Own Face in the Pond

I sent some of these pages to AKR. He corrected and edited my writings. In fact, he gave me a lecture: 'A name is like a mantra. Grandchildren are given the same name as their grandfathers. Ancient names are given to the children of today. In some African tribes, the day of one's rebirth is the day of one's naming ceremony. When a chieftain dies, his name dies too, and along with it, they rename all things connected with the chief and his name. So much so, if an epidemic wipes out the population, the entire language gets replaced. Our ancients believed that the soul is immortal and is therefore nameless. But for these people in Africa, the name itself is the soul. It is the same for you, KKR, and for me AKR.'

'When I first met you, I too had an uneasy feeling about our identical names. It was like Narcissus seeing his own reflection. Do you know the Greek myth of Narcissus and Echo? Narcissus looked into a pool of water, and seeing his own reflection for the first time, fell in love with his own image. When he tried to make love to his own reflection, he fell in and drowned. He was oblivious of Echo, the beautiful girl who loved him. Mourning the loss of Narcissus, she wasted away disappearing as an echo. Be careful, Ramanuja! You too have an element of Narcissus in you—otherwise, why would you write an autobiography and send it to me? Don't overdo it, you may lose sight of what else is involved. Once when I was thinking of the great Swami Ramanujacharya[†] and his famous "cat" pronouncement, I could not even see a cat right in front of me.'

Writing this, he sent me another poem. See for yourself. He is like that: a poem when you stand up, a poem when you sit down! You don't have to read it though.

Male and female
white and black
a litter of kittens
crack open their eyes.

Without discrimination
the cat Tiger
picked them by
the scruff of their necks.

She was moving house
and, did the monkey
on the verandah
observing her keep silent?

And, did he drop
from a high branch
while thinking of
another Ramanujan?

By which time
our cat Tiger had
disappeared from view
with her entire brood.

Chapter Thirteen

High Court by the Shore

My elder brother-in-law lived in Purasavaakkam. He was a tall man with a shaven dome for a head, shining black. His name was Gopalan, the same as my brother's. From 1940–2 he was well settled in Burma, working in a bank. When the Japanese attacked, he and others fled at night, walking through thorny thickets and jungles to reach Calcutta as refugees. He had sent his family off to India before the Japanese invasion. He was not talkative about those old days; he carried himself with old-world dignity, rare these days. He bathed upon waking, went upstairs to the verandah, picked up the shree churna box and carefully, in front of a hand-held mirror, marked his forehead. Then he recited the 'Prayer of a Thousand Names' addressed to Lord Vishnu.[†] Since I slept on the verandah, his prayers woke me.

That evening I engaged him in a philosophical debate. He was taken with the notion of karma. Having read Bertrand Russell, I was a sceptic whose only certainty was scepticism. I don't remember the topic of our debate. I am like a police dog going after a single whiff; I am pursuing each smell from the past. I don't remember the dry patches of our talk. Like a real police dog that neither knows nor cares about the minute details of the case or the modus operandi of an investigator, my chase tends to follow each scent. What I do remember is that it was a Saturday.

On Monday of that week, Appa had to visit someone in the high court and he took me with him. It was a huge, red-brick building built in the British colonial style. In its dimly lit hall, there were slowly revolving fans. They hung from the high ceilings, like bats dangling from cables. The benches along the wall were worn and polished smooth over a hundred years by thousands of plaintiffs, defendants, and families waiting anxiously. Above each bench, a wide swathe of the wall more than fifteen feet long showed grease stains from heads roiled in turmoil, pressed against the wall, waiting for their cases and pending appeals in the ever slow-moving court. Bespectacled advocates in black gowns and white turbans hopped around like ravens.

Appa had gone to the court to meet one Mr Srinivasa Iyengar, another son-in-law of his elder brother. When he saw me, Mr Iyengar said, 'Hello, Ramanja! You have come to the court. Ha, ha, ha.' His laughter was loud. He rang a bell for his peon to fetch coffee from the canteen. Father moved close to Iyengar, took out some papers from his pocket and showed him neatly written notes, speaking in a whisper; the subject of their talk was obviously not for my ears. But the lawyer replied in a booming voice, with no concerns whatsoever as to who heard what.

I drank the dirty-brown watery coffee the peon brought us in black china cups. On the walls were framed law certificates and twenty-year-old group photographs of members of the High Court Bar Association, and a calendar with Lord Krishna[†] playing the flute. On each certificate and group picture, I looked for Srinivasa Iyengar's name and face. In the early shots he stood in the back row with thirty others, wearing a narrow turban and a thick black jacket, appearing no more than a staring head among others at the rear. In other photographs over the years, he had grown fatter, wore black glasses, and was gradually moving forward into front rows. In the final year's picture, though he was not in the dead centre, he sat proudly on the fourth chair from the middle. He now wore a single red mark on his forehead, instead of the traditional three. He no longer wore his earrings; instead, he wore gold-rimmed glasses. Gray hair jetted out from around his ears and from under the turban. In another photograph he sat on a platform with the famous singer M. S. Subbalaxmi, the mayor of Madras, and other celebrities; he could be seen wearing a long advocate's gown, a silk turban and an embroidered scarf. I saw him smiling in only one of the photographs, and I could see a gold crown on his canine tooth.

At two in the afternoon when we came out that day, it had been cloudy. From the court's window I saw the ocean turning into a slate colour. That was the first time I had seen the sea. That night I had a closer view.

(AKR commented that since my 'description of the sea is not different from one of the eighteen traditional descriptions, it would be better to skip it', and I have done so.)

On one of those three nights (I'm not sure which), we went to Thiruvellikkeni for dinner. Appa was born and raised in that old house. His sister-in-law, her daughter, and son-in-law lived in one portion of that house, subletting the rest of the house to other young families. The house was dark, and it had the same smell as all old houses, but there was also an enticing smell of a delicate Madras rasam[†] and payasam[†] that Doddamma[†] had prepared from recipes handed down for generations. We spent the night there.

It was an unbearably hot night. My bed and pillows reeked stale. Upstairs in a small room, the three male members of the family slept under a fan. I hardly slept. Because of the moonlight, they had turned off the street lights. Other than the sound of men's snoring and the cricket's chirpings, the night was silent.

In the middle of the silence, though, I kept hearing an unfamiliar rise and lull of something thunderous, seemingly coming from nowhere and very like the roar of tigers at the zoo in Mysore. I thought, it couldn't have been the sound of thunder, since it was a cloudless moonlit night. After a long time I realized that I was listening to the roar of the Madras sea coming from a block away. Only in the middle of the night when the noise of the people had quietened down, could the eternal roar of the ocean be heard.

When I got up to take a piss, I looked through the window and didn't expect to see much of an ocean from there: but I did. Spread across the blue horizon's edge, there it was, between two rows of houses on two sides of a street, I saw the sea shining like mercury in the moonlight.

I doubt if those houses were there when Appa was young; he must have grown up with the sound and sight of the vast ocean.

Chapter Fourteen

A Spot Where Appa Sat in 1918

The loiterers outside the high court could be seen everywhere: under the trees, on benches, standing, sitting, sleeping. Vendors sold sliced cucumber sprinkled with red chili and pepper, cubed bright yellow papayas, and roasted peanuts. Appa took me to a restaurant across from the court and bought *rava dosa*,[†] coffee, and badami halwa.[†] He rarely went to restaurants. After those three days in Madras, he would take me on long walks a few times a year, and once in a while, he would buy me fruit salad or superb dosas[†] from Indra Bhawan. I have been to Indra Bhavan many times since then and ordered the same fruit salad and dosa, to relive the experience, but such attempts are bound to be disappointing.

Going back to Purasavaakkam this time we took a bus. Near the municipal building on Mount Road there was a white statue of a British governor on horseback with a hand stretched skyward. His prancing mount had a foreleg in the air. Even before we reached the statue, Appa said, 'In 1918, after a big quarrel with my Anna,[†] I came here and sat under that statue.' For a second I was startled. I wondered—does Appa ever quarrel? That too, with Doddappa, his elder brother, who had raised him, sent him to school and seen to it that he earned his BA; Doddappa for whom Appa felt great respect and reverence. How could Appa have quarrelled with him? I have often looked at Doddappa's large signature with the two dots under his name in the heavy dictionary awarded him by the Mission High School when he was a schoolboy. Appa had even borrowed the manner of proudly placing with a flourish the two dots under his own name, same as the one under Doddappa's signature. Only one of my brothers has taken to signing as they did, placing two dots under his own signature. This brother of mine even looks a bit like Appa. The same nose, the same mouth, the same eyes.

When the bus came to Mount Road, I looked at Appa and said, 'Why did you quarrel with your brother?'

'Because of her, your Atthe, the one you saw yesterday,' he said.

'What did she do?'

'She and my Atthige[†] always schemed from the kitchen, plotting one thing or the other. One day, they complained that one of the two gold chains from the chest of drawers had disappeared,' Appa said.

I wondered where the chain went, who would have taken it. No one knows to this day. Doddappa got incensed about the missing chain. Atthe told Doddappa that Appa was seen rummaging in the drawers. Like grandfather, Doddappa too was hot-tempered. When he was angered, he did not distinguish between a leg and a head, as they say. That day, he shouted and yelled at Appa, standing right at the front door near the street. Then Appa became angry too. Needless to say, he had not stolen the gold chain. Why would he steal? He had received his BA degree, and though it was still summer holidays, he had found a teaching post at the European High School, and he was married to Amma (though she had not yet begun living with him). He said to Doddappa, 'Do you rule over your empire by listening to what these women are saying? I can't live here any longer.'

He packed his clothes in a suitcase, and without even finishing his meal, he washed his hands and went out of Doddappa's home. Appa could hear Doddappa shouting, 'Is this how you pay me back for all those things that I have done for you? Each drop of blood that is flowing in your body is from the kavala[†] I served. I took into my home a cobra, and I offered it milk!'

Those were to be the final words he would hear from his brother as he left that house. I am sure Appa must have been quite upset and hesitant at first. But he had already passed the threshold. Atthe and his Athige had not uttered a single word during the quarrel, not even when Appa went out of the house. I suspect that the two women had stolen the chain themselves and hidden it somewhere. They were always into some sort of secret chit fund or savings scheme. Doddappa's wife had a brother, a rogue of a shiftless man, who came in through the back door and borrowed money from his sister. Well, Appa left his brother's house that day with a single suitcase. He sat all afternoon under the statue of the horseman, the very statue we were passing. Though I was young when Appa told me this story, I felt very sorry for him. My stomach burned.

Appa had no friends then. He had never stayed in hotels. All he had was sixteen rupees and six annas. With that he bought himself a bus ticket and went to Madhurai to his sister's place. From there he went on to Mysore for an interview, found a job, and lived there his remaining years. Appa said, 'The first World War had ended. In 1918, Mahatma Gandhi had already been back in India three or four years. During that time, neither my brother nor I had ever been angry.'

I have told you already that Appa's first marriage took place in 1916. Amma was his second wife. Though she had told me the date of their wedding, for many years I had secretly suspected that my parents were lying to me about my elder brother, Gopi; I thought that he was actually my stepbrother, a son of Appa's by his first wife, and not through Amma.

In 1918, Appa's first wife lived with him only for a few months in Mysore and she died the next year during childbirth. She was sixteen and pretty. She had a perfect classical nose as in ancient Greek statuary. She could even sing well. Her eyebrows met in the middle (which feature, I am told, brings good luck). Her long hair came down to her ankles. Appa kept repeating all these things about his first wife to us and to Amma, again and again, so much so that Amma developed an inferiority complex about herself. Her nose was flat and broad, and her face was Dravidian. Appa would tease her even in his old age; thirty years into their married life, he would say, 'I charged 500 rupees dowry just for that nose.' Amma's face would droop, her nose appearing even flatter.

Chapter Fifteen

The Two Ghosts

The unhoused soul of Appa's first wife haunted Amma, who must have felt the dead wife's tormenting presence for many years. Amma spoke of it forty years later, as we waited for the train to Coimbatore[†] at the Bangalore station.

'Those who marry for a second time tend to put their first wives on a pedestal. That is why no one should let a daughter marry a man who had been married earlier. It is even worse if the man had children by his first wife. You remember the Sankethi Brahmin,[†] the high school teacher? Soon after his wife of thirty years died, he went off to a village and married the twenty-year-old daughter of a poor man. Was he in a hurry! The schoolteacher already had a son of sixteen who quarrelled every day with his new stepmother. The old man began to distrust his own son. After he married me, Appa too kept praising his first wife. He would say, her nose was so pretty, her eyes were like this, she was so slim, so tall, and he would show how tall she was against the cupboard. Even if he felt all that, he didn't have to go on about it to me. He may have meant to tease me, but it pained me. It was a game for him. As they say, "What is play for the cat is death for the rat."'

'After Gopi was born in 1923, I developed a high fever in the hospital. I thought I might die then, along with our first-born son, just like Appa's first wife. For three days in a row I thought I saw the muttaide,[†] the ghost of Appa's first wife, wearing an old sari, standing as tall as the cupboard in the kitchen, stretching her hands towards me, near my bed, begging, pleading, "Yes, yes, give me. Give me." I would shut my eyes and wake up screaming.'

Just then the train we had been waiting for arrived. We got in and found our seats. The train began moving, leaving behind plants and trees, houses, villages, and station after lantern-waving station. With the train sounding its whistle and making the 'gada da, gada da' sound through the night, Amma continued telling me the story.

'One hot day at noon, everything looked white. The hospital bed, the walls, the uniformed nurses, and even the sky all became bleached white. As I nursed Gopi at my breast, I happened to glance up and I saw her right there in front of me. It was *She* all right and none other. Her hair was dishevelled. She said, "Give me your kumkum. That baby is mine, give him to me." She leaned forward to grab my son. I clutched my six-day-old Gopi, shut my eyes tightly, held on to my mangalsutra and prayed to the Lord of Thirupathi.† I looked again, opened my eyes and found her wide-set, obsessed eyes staring at me. Gathering her streaming uncombed hair and twisting it into a coil at the back of her head, she took a few steps backwards and flew through the lattice on the window. The apparition had vanished into thin air. I clearly remember that her feet never touched the ground.'

'For the next three days I ran a high fever. I begged the doctors and nurses to let me go home, but they said, "It is not uncommon for women to lose their minds temporarily after delivery. Don't be scared. You mustn't believe in demons and ghosts. We'll give you some medicine." They gave me sleeping pills. But that very night, the dead woman came back with dishevelled hair and kumkum spread over her forehead; she laid her hands on me and shook me. She tried to grab and pull at my mangalsutra. For a fleeting moment, I thought this was happening in a dream. But, then, as soon as I opened my eyes, I saw her clearly. From a corner window, her body was swaying in the moonlight. She was like smoke rising against the light. Her evil intention had stamped a crazy expression on her face. Her long, uncombed, flowing, dark hair came down to her ankles; curly tendrils of hair moved across her forehead; her eyes were bright. Her icy cold hands grabbed my neck, and I shouted with all my strength, "Ayyyyo! Leave me. Leave me alone!" I was so frightened! I was not yet sixteen. When the nurses came running in, the ghost had gone through the window, just as she had done earlier. Later, when I told anyone about it, no one believed me. They gave me a shot in the buttock and put me to sleep.'

'Three days later, one Bhagirathamma came to see me in the hospital. You know her, Ramu. She is the midwife who helped me deliver you and the other children at home.'

I said, 'Oh, yes, that woman, with the clean-shaven head? Her grandson Sethu was my classmate in middle school. He had a stammer. Poor boy; other children mocked him by stuttering his name, "Se…se…se..Sethu". He would get mad and throw stones at them. They did this even when his grandmother came to the school to scold the boys.'

'Yes, the same Bhagirathamma,' Amma went on. 'Don't say "shaven-head". The poor woman. Her kind of Brahmins are stricter than ours; their widows have to shave their heads. Her husband was an LMP—a licensed medical practitioner—who died young. It seems he had gone to see a distant cousin of his who had just died. Since the dead man had no relatives, this doctor took it upon himself and arranged for the funeral. He took his purifying bath at a local pond, walked home in the hot blazing sun; he complained of a severe headache and then succumbing to a stroke, he died within three days. His wife was familiar with her husband's profession; she knew how to give injections, how to sterilize needles and syringes. The poor woman studied and earned a midwife's diploma to support herself and to pay for her son's education.'

Amma told me many such stories, speaking to me at length.

I said, 'Amma, you said that Bhagirathamma came to see you. What happened then?'

'I was about to tell you. By god's grace she came to help me when I was so ill over visitations from the dead woman. I can't mimic

Bhagirathamma. Her north-Karnataka[†] speech or her nasal voice is hard to imitate. She came to see me when she heard how the dead woman was troubling me and she said, "With the rising of the full moon, evil forces are afoot, as it was last night. When she was alive, she had no children; she died in childbirth with her desires unfulfilled. That is why she has come back as a *devva*[†] to haunt you. Now that you have a son she has come to torment you."'

'My second sister-in-law Rangubai's husband was an accountant in the mounted division of the maharaja's army. He became friends with His Highness the king and even learned to ride horses. During the Dussehra parades,[†] he would wear khaki uniforms and polished, knee-high, black boots, a police turban, a belt with a large shining buckle, and he would carry a silver-plated baton. He would accompany the King to Banni Mantap.[†] He was highly orthodox. He parted his cropped hair under his police turban, but also kept a thin juttu[†] at the back. As soon as he came home, he took a bath. He would put on his prayer dhoti[†] that had been washed and dried in the sun according to custom, he would mark his arms and forehead with sandalwood paste, and then he would offer evening prayers. The poor man had no children. He died when he was barely forty-five.

'After death he would come back as a spirit to haunt his wife, whom he had loved dearly while he was alive. On full moon nights, the dead man's devva would rise with the moon and walk right into his wife's bedroom. He would wait next to the dark wood of their bridal bed, which was given to them as her dowry from her father. The devva wore the same khaki uniform and tall, black riding boots that was the uniform of the soldiers on horseback. He still wore his yellow sapphire studs. The neighbours clearly heard the "thump, thump, thump" sound of the marching boots as he came in and went out of the house. Sometimes the devva would order her about, saying, "Take off my shoes. Bring me my dhoti." Some nights he would demand that she sleep with him. The poor woman was so scared even to look up. She would bolt herself in the kitchen or bathroom, cowering and trembling. Once he was filled with a fit of jealousy and yelled at her, saying, "In front of me you act as if you were a shy grieving widow with that shaven head and the rest. This afternoon you stood near the window, listening to the love song, *Ha Priya Prashantha Hrudaya*,[†] that your neighbour was playing. You ought to be ashamed. These days even widows don't mind going after lovers."'

'Her hardships increased; she suffered without relief, and she prayed to Lord Hanuman.[†] To protect herself, she was able to get a specially consecrated holy charm. She fasted on Thursdays. She even thought of going away to escape such torment from her dead husband's devva. Do you know what happened? One full-moon night when he returned with the sound of marching boots she decided to confront him boldly, come what may. "Why are you treating me like this? Have I not performed your funeral rites properly? I invited all those Brahmins to pray for your soul. Am I not the one who married you with Agni[†] as our witness, thirty years ago? Did I ever deceive you? You were like a god to me; wasn't losing you enough of a tragedy? If your soul has not yet found peace in your afterlife, I will jump in a well and become a devva and join you." She cried, begged, pleaded. The devva caressed her back and her shaven head. He looked at her with compassion, turned around, and once again went out in style, with the resounding tread of his riding boots. He never returned again. She still lives in Malleswaram.[†] She is in her eighties and blind.'

'Then Bhagirathamma advised me, "Jayamma, I am telling you all this for a reason. When the first wife comes again, do not get scared. Speak to her face-to-face, as if she were alive. See what happens." That was her advice to me; Bhagirathamma is a great person.'

'That night I held the baby in my arms. The moonlight was not so bright. For some reason, the baby refused to suckle. I looked up and once again, saw the dead wife with her long hair and I could hear her whisper, "Give me your kumkum. Your baby is mine. Give it to me." I held up my son, and showed the baby to her. "Take a good look. See, he looks like a prince, doesn't he? Will he survive, if you snatch him away? This is your baby. I am like your sister. Don't torture us. Protect us. Guard this family. When he grows up, this boy will offer prayers to the goddess in the temple in your name. He is your son too. Let him live," I begged her looking straight into her eyes. She heard me. Staring back at my baby and me, she did not even blink her eyelids. She withdrew her outstretched arms, lifted her hands over her head, made a sweeping motion to gather and twist her hair into a knot over her head. Then, as if blown by a current of air, she moved backwards and flew out through the window. This time too, her feet did not touch the floor. At that moment, I found her to be pretty and graceful. I was deeply saddened by her sorrow and her loss, but my fever subsided. She never came back, nor did she ever bother us again.'

Unable to contain my curiosity, I said, 'What was her name?' Amma looked away, her eyes filled. She pulled her sari around her shoulders and tightened her nose-ring. The hurtling train ran through the night. I watched the reflection of drowsy passengers in the train window.

To this day I do not know that woman's name and Appa never spoke about her.

Chapter Sixteen

What Americans Fear

Next morning, I woke up to the sound of Gopal Iyengar's recitation of Lord Vishnu's 'Prayer of a Thousand Names'. He was near my bed; he cupped his hands so he could peer at the sun through the space between his fingers. I was wide awake. I could only see the red border of his dhoti and his left foot. He too had a touch of elephantiasis, but it was less severe than Atthe's. He was forty or forty-five and must have come down with it a few years earlier. Although his left foot appeared bigger compared to the right, it wasn't like Atthe's huge swollen foot; there was just a small bulge behind the toes of the foot that looked like a loaf baking in the oven. The skin had no wrinkles. As we drank coffee he told Appa, 'I have had this trouble for years now. First I thought it came from the contaminated water in Madras. But some doctors told me that I had filaria. It turned out to be so. I have the "elephant-leg" as they say in Malaya and Burma. A mosquito must have bitten me fifteen years ago when I was in Burma. The worm incubated and stayed dormant in my body all these years, only to act up now, in my forties. That's how some diseases develop in our body. They say even cancer is like that—being dormant for twenty or thirty years, it finds an opportunistic moment to make its presence felt. Then it spreads rapidly, eating away the victim, taking over the body within a year.'

It was very like those villains who steal up on their victims in detective novels. Amma once said, 'If you step on a cobra, it stalks and finds you even after twelve years to exact its revenge.' I was not sure what crime we had committed against these filaria germs.

On hearing Gopal Iyengar had elephantiasis, Appa began to worry and became alarmed. He wanted to know more, asked more questions, and Gopal Iyengar obliged him.

'There are two kinds of mosquito, as you know. One sits at an angle on the wall. This is called the Anopheles—the one that brings malaria. The other is the Culex variety, which sits with its body parallel on the wall. Have you observed them, Ramu?' he said, turning in my direction. I had first heard of it years earlier somewhere in school. Later I learned that only the female mosquito transmits the germs of this disease. It needs to drink blood to gain energy to reproduce. In any case, from that day onwards, before I took a swat at any mosquito, I tried to check out how it sat against a wall or on my leg, to study the angle of its filament legs that were so delicate.

Recently, I saw a Culex mosquito again in a small American town. It was a hot summer day. I was near a patch of damp grass in front of a pretty pond. A row of mallards floated across the pond looking for fish. Brown finger-sized fish swam near me. Peacock-coloured, ugly ducks with touches of iridescence turned in anticipation of breadcrumbs as I casually glanced their way. There were dragonflies over the grass and suddenly I saw one mosquito—right in front of me, a Culex! I was alarmed. I thought this mosquito might bite a fish and give it an elephantiasis leg. Then I realized, of course, fish don't have feet. I was relieved! Though I reassured myself that filarial parasites are not found in America, I was suddenly concerned that I might have been infected twenty years earlier, and I feared that it would show up any time soon in my forties.

Over the next three or four days, I felt as if my legs were getting heavier. I pressed the top of my foot with a finger to check for an indentation from swelling. I remembered Appa laughing wickedly, as if it were a joke, and saying, 'When elephantiasis affects the scrotum, it swells like a balloon. Then, when out walking, a man needs a baby stroller to carry his own swollen balls.' Whenever my groin would itch even slightly or became red or swollen from ant bites at picnics,

I would scratch the spot and be overcome with anxiety thinking that the filarial germs were acting up. I was afraid that one day I might have to buy a baby stroller to carry my balls, even before having my own babies.

Gopal Iyengar gave Appa another lesson on elephantiasis. 'After the germs mature, once a month along with the full moon, the disease brings high fevers. You must then monitor the fever by an hourly measurement of temperature using a thermometer. Why do you think I always keep a thermometer? Precisely at the hour of midnight, these germs lay thousands of eggs in the blood stream, bringing you fever. By one in the morning the body feels about four degrees warmer than normal, but by three the fever subsides; everything then returns to normal. So, you may not even be aware that you have the filaria germs in your body. Establishing the condition is like detective work. One must stalk it at midnight and catch it,' Gopal Iyengar explained, exactly as I might have. He said, it was like the ebb and flow of the Madras sea; his old body had a way of repeating itself in a recurring rhythm.

You may wonder, 'Why is this man writing all this?' Now, in my thirty-eighth year, I am suddenly concerned that my leg may get swollen from the polluted waters of Madras. This is the same kind of phobia from which Americans suffer.

I have not told any of this to my wife yet. She may even seek a divorce, fearing that I have in my body this parasite. After all, she is an American. I am also afraid to see a doctor. In this country, you can talk freely about your venereal diseases, but if you even suggest the possibility of a communicable disease caught in the tropics, the news gets undue coverage and becomes the subject of frightening headlines. If they thought I have elephantiasis, they might even quarantine me. The police searched all over the country for Typhoid Mary who is said to have brought typhoid into America.

You might not even find cures for filaria in America because it is a disease of foreign origin. The doctors will do hundreds of tests and possibly consider me to be a hazard to public health. They might revoke my visa and deport me. People in America are so scared of germs from foreign countries they don't even let us bring in a mango from India. Now, if they see me dragging my feet I may face the same fate as did that man in Madhurai.

One day in Madhurai I was travelling in a TVS Bus. The TVS bus looked like a box made of faded tin foil. The buses were always punctual; if it was supposed to arrive at the Cliff-Massy stop by 11:12, you could count on its being there exactly on time, not late by even one second. My bus was headed towards the Teppa Pond, which was the final stop at the edge of town. There were no more than fifteen passengers in the bus. The weather was not too hot. As the bus made the turn around the temple's golden gopuram tower,[†] I looked back and saw the row of stone pillars with sculpted carvings of horses inside the temple corridor. I even remember seeing the sculpture of Nandi, the holy bull. When the bus came near Market Street, I was thrilled how fantastic this fabled old city was—a city of temples. Its warm sunshine, the stupendous temple gopurams, towers, and its people dressed in white all looked so wonderful. The bus stopped just for a second at the Jaya Theatre stop before moving on.

Suddenly I sensed that there was a change in the mood of those passengers. Their facial expressions had changed. They seemed scared, though I couldn't see why. The conductor stood up suddenly, blew his whistle, and shouted at the driver, 'Stop, stop!' He turned towards a passenger who was just then boarding the bus; the man had cropped hair and was wearing a spotless, bright white shirt and dhoti. The conductor yelled at him with contempt, displaying no respect whatsoever, 'Chee, Chee, Chee! Get out! Get out of the bus, right now! This very minute!' He kept a safe distance from the man, but still managed to get him off the bus. The ejected passenger's face looked like a mask of red wood. The skin over his nose, cheeks, and eyes was red and swollen.

A man in his long coat next to me said, 'Lepers, lepers…! Don't they have special colonies? With lepers out on the roads, what will become of us?'

Another man in white cotton clothes said, 'Of course there are leper colonies, but this leper has crores.[†] He bribes the officials and stays out of the leper colonies. He gets on these buses simply to annoy us, and to see how we react. It is just play for him. He has two cars.'

Who knew if that was true or not, but the conductor said, 'I don't care if he has crores! Thank god, he did not sit in the bus. If he did, we would have had to use phenoyl to cleanse that spot.'

A man chewing betel leaves said, 'Thank goodness the bus was not crowded!'

I have heard it said that lepers have a face like that of a lion. It was then that I realized exactly what it meant.

You can understand why I was now worried about people thinking of me as having elephantiasis. I might also be treated the same way as that poor leper in Madhurai. I would have to buy a larger pant to hide my leg, but then I would need a giant-sized shoe. How can I have the shoe made secretly? A pair of shoes of different sizes for each foot! How disgusting! I bought a thermometer and secretly monitored my temperature day and night. But there were no signs of filaria. Sometimes my body temperature was even lower than 98 degrees!

During the week of the rising moon, I would wake up quietly and get out of bed around midnight. I secretly checked my body temperature, being careful not to wake my wife. When the temperature did not budge even by a single degree, I felt ashamed and silly. I would then feel as if my engorged leg was getting better. It was good that I didn't tell this to anybody. America! America!

Each country has its fears. In my own land, we are afraid of typhoid, malaria, and the like, but here in America people live in fear of cancer and a variety of new diseases. There, we are afraid of falling ill, getting sick; here they are also afraid of being afraid. There, we worry about germs; here they worry about being overdosed with extremely powerful drugs. In the 1960s, pregnant women took thalidomide prescribed as sleeping pills and produced deformed babies, more than 10,000 of them, with no arms and legs, only a head and torso. Still those children looked so smart and lovely. They didn't suffer from elephant-legs. They had no legs! They learned to write using their teeth. If they had feet, they used their toes to fetch dropped pencils from the floor. This is the sort of worry that afflicts Americans. People like me, Indians in America, suffer from both brands of anxieties. We suffer the burdens of both cultures.

Was my leg really swollen? Was my obsession about relatives with filaria simply the reason for my anxiety to express itself through my body? Or, was it my dormant filarial disease flaring up now and, in the process, bringing back my repressed memories of Madras? This is a cycle: from mind to body to mind.

An American friend of my wife tells us often that one must look at one's body to figure out one's mind. It seems that her psychiatrist advised her on how she was to handle her dilemmas about her impending divorce.

He said to his patient, 'Here is an exercise that may help you. If your mind is inclined to say "Yes", bend your left thumb; if it is inclined to say "No", do not bend it. Do this exercise ten times.' He helped her to practise this.

Once when her husband was away, she had an occasion to sleep with another man. She was unsure what to do. She called her psychiatrist for advice and said, 'I think that I should not go out with him tonight. Yet, somehow there is this desire; he is tall and handsome. My husband is not in town.'

The psychiatrist said, 'What does your left thumb say?' The patient saw that her left thumb was bent. Her conflict was resolved by her left thumb. For the dilemma in her mind, she had an answer in her thumb.

In my search to find my atma,[†] I began to write. I thought it would help me find my self, and it has ended with the body. This autobiography has become ridiculous. It reminds me of my absent-minded teacher. He kept looking for his eyeglasses; he was searching for his spectacles with the help of those very lenses riding on his nose. Cannot the body's nine orifices open up and give us a glimpse of Lord Krishna's place of birth? May we not consider each orifice to be an opening in the wall of a temple, as in the legend about the untouchable saint Kanaka,[†] who sat outside the temple, singing? Didn't the saint's voice shatter the temple wall creating a hole in the wall with his singing?

Such matters when put into words appear ridiculous. I may seem to be free-associating and I may appear to be telling you unrelated matters. But what can you expect from someone like me who has studied from childhood: such diverse texts as mantras addressed to gods, the writings of the mendicant poets, the hymns of the Alvars,[†] the kirtanas of Thyagaraja,[†] Appa's recitals of the Bhagavadgita, and in school with friends, the works of Basava,[†] Kumaravyasa, Kuvempu, Bendre, Ramakrisna, and others. Why wouldn't this Dwaraka,[†] this Krishna, this Kanaka,[†] this patchwork of images, all appear in this autobiography I am writing?

Chapter Seventeen

Memories of a Psychophage

This body too is a genetic, biological patchwork. The mind is a hotchpotch of things heard or read or learned. Inside us we hoard gestures and images from persons unknown, and when we look into the medley, we realize that we are not ourselves. We are the twisted tortured shreds and patches of other lives. A song you heard somewhere years ago in a bus may suddenly come back to you, and you may not be able to get rid of it. I cannot sing, but so often when I am alone in a faraway city in some other part of the world, I may suddenly remember *Krishna nee begane baro*,[†] a song from the Bala Saraswathi[†] dance-drama, staged in the Mysore Town Hall. I begin to hum its tune and keep time by moving my neck as musicians do. My wife teases me at parties, 'My husband knows only one tune: hmmm-hmmm-hmmmhmmm uhhhh-uhhh-uhhh-uhhh. He hums it to himself even on the street.'

After watching the Japanese movie *Yojimbo*,[†] I was so impressed by the heavy, leg-lifting gait of its six-foot-tall hero that for a couple of days I started imitating him. But, soon I realized that I was at least six inches shorter than he was and my imitation of his gait looked silly and ridiculous.

When husband and wife live together day and night, they end up imitating each other so that, over time, their thoughts and actions begin to look very much like each other's. By the time they get old, they look like clones.

Take my elderly professor of history at the university, Subba Ramayya and his wife. She was a typical Karnataka[†] woman. Born in a village near Arakalagoodu,[†] she wore a large kumkum on her forehead, kept her pepper and salt hair well groomed. She couldn't speak English. She loved her husband dearly. Whenever she openly complimented him, he would blush. Once during the year-end party for the senior students of the history honours class, she was talking in a loud voice with my classmate Prema, 'You don't know how many books my husband reads! He cooks the best onion stew. During the three days of my monthly periods, it was he who always cooked. The food used to taste so good that I looked forward to my periods. Now that I have passed that age, of course, I am missing his onion sambar for dinner.'

Subba Ramayya, embarrassed, blushed under his gray hair. 'Chee, stop it,' he said under his breath, controlling his temper. Still, I was surprised. There was something romantic between them. That night, I observed the professor and his wife. His small graying eyebrows, his clean-shaven oily-plump cheeks, his tiny nose and big round eyes like that of a rhesus monkey, somehow gave his face a special kind of charm. His wife, by his side, also appeared to be just like him; she too had the same simian nose and eyes, and her face had an identical glow of loving satisfaction. After being together for forty years, each had become the mirror image of the other. When they say 'a single soul in two bodies', is this what they mean?

> If they see
> Breasts and long hair coming
> They call it woman,
> If beard and whiskers
> They call it man:
>
> But, look, the self that hovers
> In between
> Is neither man nor woman
>
> O Ramanatha

When he wrote this poem, the saint Devara Dasimayya must have had couples like Subba Ramayya and his wife in mind. Did Dasimayya come to realize the spiritual meaning of this poem later on in life? (The above poem was new to me; AKR sent it to me after reading what I wrote about mirror-resembling selves.)

Of late, my wife and I are beginning to merge like this. As I told you, she is American, born and raised in Vermont. She is one year older than me, about an inch taller and has copper-red hair, like a fine-bred horse. Her grandfather was German, her grandmother Irish. I am a Mysorian—my wavy, thick, dark Dravidian hair hangs with curls down my neck when I let it grow. Though she had been to India as a Peace Corps volunteer, she had not learned Kannada. Her taste in food, clothes, music, and such was Indian, but our mutual cultures were different. Yet we were blended together like chutney made from sea salt and mountain-nelli.† When we talked in bed, watched movies, cried together, or touched in the dark of midnight, or at dusk or dawn, or in the brightness of afternoons, as we embraced or shared body heat, I was her, and she was me. It sounds ridiculous, but it is true nonetheless. My wife dismisses this as my crazy notion from being a Hindu. I am not sure if my blood is Hindu or hers Lutheran.

In my early days of living in America, in Virginia, someone invited me for dinner. My hostess said, 'My dad lives with me too.' She must have been fifty and her father at least seventy-five.

I asked, 'Why didn't he join us for dinner?' Perhaps I shouldn't have asked.

She said, 'He doesn't generally eat with us when we have guests. He has lost his memory. Now, like a baby, he has no control over his body,' which meant that he needed diapers.

Usually in America old people like this don't stay with their children. They are admitted to nursing homes and children visit them weekly or monthly. For us who fuss so much over our parents, this seems very sad and cruel. I think it is much better among the Eskimos. Friends and relatives take their elderly out of the village, far away into the snow-covered wilderness where they leave them. The elderly walk away, slowly, deliberately, with dignity like an elephant, to die quietly, alone in solitude under the sky, close to mother earth. Such a respectable honourable way to go.

Unlike others, it was very caring of this lady to have kept her father with her and to have cared about him.

'Do you want to see him?' she asked.

'Let's see him,' I said.

She took me to the basement and tapped on an oak door. 'Come in,' said a rough voice from inside. We went into a panelled room. Amid the musty odour of medicine sat an extremely old, tiny man near a huge table, over which hung a stained-glass Tiffany lamp. He wore a skullcap and didn't even look up. He would forget what happened the minute before. From a pile of jigsaw puzzle pieces he was busy assembling a large, half-finished puzzle of President Lincoln that stretched over most of the table. I had not seen such a large likeness of Lincoln before. The old man had already completed Lincoln's tall hat, bushy eyebrows, and wide forehead. He had done the left side of the beard, the deep-set left eye, and part of the nose. The right cheek, right eye, and the rest had yet to be completed. He had to sift through hundreds of pieces to match the angles, colours, and lines to finish the details of Lincoln's face. Even a single missing piece would ruin the face. When we entered, the old man exclaimed, 'Ha!' He had found a red-black, clover-shaped piece to complete Lincoln's right nostril and four strands of Lincoln's black beard.

The old man looked at me and said, 'Who is this? John's friend? Looks like a Negro,' and went on with his puzzle.

During much of the day he slept in the bed next to the table; the first thing every morning he would start solving the puzzle. There was an attached bathroom and a small TV in a corner. Five years earlier his granddaughter had given him the puzzle as a Christmas gift. Two years later, his great-granddaughter, a mischievous little girl, played with the puzzle when the old man was away. She dropped the board on the floor scattering the pieces and then ran upstairs with a handful of Lincoln's face. For weeks they found the pieces scattered almost everywhere in the house and some were sucked up by the vacuum cleaner. The daughter had to go to several stores before she found an identical one. The old man had to start all over again to do the puzzle, but his condition deteriorated. Over time, he began to lose control of his body; his memory and eyesight worsened. Now he needed eyeglasses thick as a soda bottle. He took short walks near the house, watched some TV, but mostly kept working on the puzzle. He spoke very little.

Amma used to say that when one gets that old, the mind is gone. When she went to see one of her uncles once, she found that he had dementia. At eleven o'clock in the night he would complain, 'They don't give me hot water for a bath.' Grandmother too lost her mind by the time she died. She tried to keep people away saying, 'Don't come near me, don't; I am not clean. I am having my periods.' She then would remember her mother giving her sugarcane juice and jaggery for good luck on the day of her first menstrual period.

It seems that an old lady in my wife's family too lost her mind in the final moments of her life. As they carried her to the ambulance, she said, 'What is that next to you? Is it a devil?'

They said, 'Oh, that is a tree, our apple tree, mother, can't you see?'

'Who needs a tree? I don't want it. Cut it down, cut....'

She died, even before finishing the sentence.

As I said, my hostess introduced me to her father. He did not even take a good look at me. Perhaps his hearing was poor too. Before leaving his room, I stood near his table and saw the half-finished face of Lincoln; the panelling in the room; a Jesse James poster which his children, now in college, must have hung; banners from their schools; and a Vietnam War button saying, *Make Love, Not War*.

On a display shelf there was a slightly worn-out baby shoe made of metal, not leather. Its bright, gold-coloured metallic shine, its shoestrings and folded creases, all could be seen with precise detail. My friend said, 'This is the shoe John wore when he was two. We had this made in 1942 when we were in a museum in New Orleans. They had a machine containing molten metal in which you could drop an object to turn it into a souvenir. We had just bought John a pair of new shoes, so we decided to have it made into a keepsake. This room was his room then.'

'How old is John now?' I asked.

'Twenty-eight. Seems like yesterday,' she said.

I was narrating this episode to someone the other day and suddenly my wife's expression grew dark, as if I had done something wrong. That night we had a huge quarrel.

'You steal all my stories and experiences and use them as though they were yours. That old man in Virginia? He was my friend Rita Thomas's father—you never went to Virginia. I met them so many times and told you all about them. The old man's room, its smell, the jigsaw puzzle, everything. But, the picture was not of Lincoln—it was a Taj Mahal puzzle. I even told you how surprised I was seeing Taj Mahal in their house. I shouldn't tell you anything. You don't know what to do with your own experience, but you borrow my ears and eyes and use them, and tell everyone as if they were yours. This is how men eat other men. You are a psychophage!'

However, on so many occasions she has used my jokes, even my father's words that I had heard while in Mysore; and if I repeated them and told them again, she would jump up and down, claiming that they were originally hers! As if she had the copyright and I was plagiarizing her. After my words transferred from my mouth to her mind, she would stamp my words with her approval, and sell them back to me—like Imperial Britain did. They would buy raw cotton at cheap prices from us, the Indians, transport it to England, make it into textiles in Manchester, bring it back to India and sell us the finished cloth at exorbitant prices, undercutting our own workers.

I may be like that, too. It is hard to say which is mine and which is not. The Irish poet Yeats would dream one half of his dreams in his sleep and finish off the other half in his wife's sleep.

Chapter Eighteen

Shadow Selves

As I said, for me it is hard to tell where my experiences end and my wife's begin, merged as we are. A friend once told me a story that he had heard somewhere or maybe he had a relative with identical twins. The two boys could not be told apart; not just in their features or their build, even their voices were identical. Their mother had to dress them in different colours, day and night, to tell them apart. When they were about ten, one morning they switched clothes. That day, teachers and classmates could not tell who was who. The twins had a remarkable inner connection. When one of them was drinking tea, the other said to the mother, 'His tea needs more sugar.' I don't think this is true, someone made this up.

I knew one Mr Venkata Rao in Bangalore. He was always talking about twins. One day as Krishnappa and I were about to leave a cafeteria in Gandhi Bazar, Venkata Rao came up from behind and said to Krishnappa without even a salutation, 'Did your wife deliver as yet?'

'No, sir. No. It's a behemoth pregnancy! Her belly is larger than that of Ganapathy.† Even while taking a short walk she feels exhausted and has to stop. The doctor told me last week she may be carrying twins and he asked me to keep the news from her, so she won't worry. Occasionally, he could hear two sets of fetal heartbeats. There was still time, he would do more tests, the doctor said. He managed to scare me,' said Krishnappa.

Venkata Rao said, 'With twins there will be complications, problems about clothes and problems about who they are. Each twin would want his own identity. Dogs and pigs give birth to whole litters, but unlike us, their pups don't ask, "Who am I? Who is my brother?"' Venkata Rao said that he remembered a story about twins and proceeded to tell it; it turned out to be a very long story.

He told us that some fifty years ago in Closepet,[†] a prostitute gave birth to a pair of twins. People made fun of her. They said, with so many fathers, it is surprising that she had only two! These twins were not like other twins. While among other twins one sibling might boast that his brother is four minutes older, these twins could not do that because they were not born separately. He said, 'The labour was hard and prolonged. First, one head came out, followed by two hands. Instead of the trunk and other parts coming, there was another head, and then there were two more hands! Then came two chests, two bellies, and four legs. The mother must have felt as if her womb would burst open, delivering these babies. Even before she had realized the oddity of what she was about to bring forth, the woman died from exhaustion and haemorrhage. This caused more problems. Since the dead woman couldn't push the twins out, two midwives had to tug at the babies for a long time, as in a tug-of-war game at school. I don't know whether to tell you whether one child was born or two. There were two heads, four arms, and four legs, but the two girls were twins conjoined at the hips. They cried with the force of four lungs.'

'The babies were fostered by the two sisters of the prostitute who took turns nursing them. When one of the babies was feeding at the breast, the other had to be held and comforted.'

'As they were growing up, more problems came at each step. How to walk? How to use a lavatory? What dresses? As they started taking their first steps, they had to be taught how to keep pace with each other, as in a three-legged race. Somehow they managed to learn all that. When one of them had to use the lavatory, the other would wait patiently till her sister finished. Where can you find a lavatory with two toilets properly spaced for two of them to use at the same time? They quarrelled in the bathroom. They suffered all the childhood

A. K. RAMANUJAN

ailments together, and not just colds, fevers, or measles. They had more troubles than anyone could imagine. They started wearing saris early. If one woke up early, she would tug at the other saying, "wake up, wake up". Both felt like the bird with the two heads in the tragic fable: one of the heads became so angry with the other that it ate a poisonous seed and died, so it could kill the other.'

Venkata Rao finished his story by saying, 'It was just like that. If they had to go somewhere, or had to stop for a short time, or even had to sleep, they could not agree on any detail. Although their bodies were joined together at the hip, each body had its own mind and personality. It was an ultimate prescription for hell on earth.'

As I listened to all this, I looked at Krishnappa. I could not tell what he was thinking. He asked a simple question, 'What did they name the twins?'

But Venkata Rao rushed on to tell much more. 'Ganga and Yamuna, or some such names were given to them. After all they were poor villagers. The girls could not even agree on who came out of the womb first. Ganga would say, "I was born first. I am your elder sister, you must respect me." Yamuna would say, "You are forever in such a hurry! You hurried and so our mother died. That doesn't make you my senior; you don't deserve any respect!" Neither had known the mother; but Yamuna blamed Ganga for their mother's death.'

'Think about it: their mother was a prostitute, they grew up among prostitutes, they've seen men. They knew a thing or two about such matters. Both must have started menstruating at the same time. What troubles! Yet, strangely enough, when it came to sex, they were considerate towards each other. Probably they would have embraced each other, if they could, but that was not possible. They would touch each other's back and chest, but perhaps this did not give them enough pleasure. When I saw them performing in the circus, holding each other's hips, they looked happy. I have seen Yamuna lovingly stroking an itching spot on Ganga's back, and Ganga directing her, "No, no, not there, Yamuna, just a bit lower. Yes, yes, there!"'

'At eighteen, they joined a circus. They must have felt that they couldn't work as prostitutes because of their abnormality. Around 1940, out of plain curiosity, a commerce student from the college who had a temporary job as an accountant in the circus went to see them in their tent. No one else was present. In unison, they called out a glad welcome to him. He was a fine and well-built young man in his twenties. They asked him to sit by them and then said, "Will you let us caress you?" Using their four hands, they caressed him, his groin and his face.'

'They kept telling him not to worry. "We won't harm you, don't worry. We'll make you happy!" Then one of them told the other sister with great affection, "Today, let him have you." But this was all very new to him. "Let me go! Let me go!" he cried out and managed to make his escape. People's preferences vary; there are some who would have loved to satisfy both sisters. At such sensuous moments, the sisters would play board games together; they would be friendly and intimate, and they would be like the rivers they were named after.'

Venkata Rao said, 'When I saw them first, they were very fat. Wearing Maharastrian ghati saris,[†] a rupee-sized kumkum mark on their forehead, and bangles, they would enter the circus arena along with the clown. The clown would peek under their sari petticoat to exclaim in mock surprise, "One or two?" '

'As the twins stood under the spotlight, the circus ringmaster would say, "One of the great wonders of the world. Two heads, four legs, four arms! Just like the mythological ganda berunda twin birds.[†] Here, we have a female berunda!" And as the drums sounded, the twins would spin around holding each other's free hips, and like a spinning top, their quadrupled arms and legs would become one leg, and one arm, and they would appear to be one whirling spinning single piece of clothing.'

'One of their acts was to sing together. Together, they would sing "Twinkle, Twinkle Little Star". They sang in a pronouncedly Kannada accent, "Tinkili, tinkili tittili shtaaroo! How ya vandaru vataroo yarroo"!

Singing, they would dance like puppets waving their hands at the twinkling stars above. I still remember them. People had lots of fun watching their act. Then the acrobats would leap and spin from one swing to the other at sixty feet above the ground, thrilling the spectators. Towards the end, the ringmaster would enter to the sound of drums and announce, "You must all be wondering how the two bodies of Yamuna and Ganga were fused into one. What you are about to see has never been seen by any human eye, anywhere in the world. See for yourself. Use your binoculars if you want." Then Ganga and Yamuna would appear in the spotlight wearing a red outfit on one half and green on the other. They would have anklets on all four legs. The sound of the drums would reach a crescendo and then the girls would remove the white scarf from around their hips. Underneath the white scarf their dresses were made with an opening wide enough at the hips through which we would be able to see for ourselves the whole area of where their smooth young hips were conjoined. There was nothing disgusting about it. Their yoking appeared to me like a fork in the tree of a trunk branching into two.'

'Rumor has it that for many years they were kept by a rich man. They must have given their master untold pleasure. In sexual matters, as I said, they never competed with each other. On such days they played happily, clapping their hands, giggling and smiling, and even if one lost to the other in a game of dice that they were playing together, they addressed each other affectionately as "Gangu" and "Yammu". According to the young circus accountant, their warmth lasted only for about an hour and during that time, they must have looked pretty and joyous.'

'It seems that they died in their youth after a bout of fever. They always had minor illnesses, but they couldn't survive a serious fever. Dying was not easy; they did not die at the same time. Ganga died first in the morning and Yamuna died in the evening. Lying in her hospital bed next to the already dead Ganga, Yamuna was half-conscious all that final day. She tried to wake up her sister, "Gangu, Gangu, akka!†

Do you want to pee?" She tried to get up, as if to go to the lavatory, but unable to lift the dead weight of her sister, she fell back. The nurses brought her a bedpan, wiped her sweat, and consoled her. If Yamuna had survived a few more days, it would have been very hard for anyone to watch. It is hard even to imagine what it must have been for her. Their bodies were separate and independent of each other only to a very small extent. I would go as far as to say, they were one person, not two.'

I suddenly remembered what a friend of mine told me once. Five days after his grandfather died, his grandmother died, unable to bear his loss.

Hearing the story of the conjoined twins, Krishnappa's lips became ashen. While telling the story, Venkata Rao had actually forgotten all about us, but suddenly realized to whom he was telling all this. He said, 'Oh, Krishnappa, this is an old story. I took almost an hour telling you! Don't be scared. Having twins is rare, and having Siamese twins is rarer still—a case in a million. Perhaps I shouldn't have told you all this!'

I said, 'How do you know all this?'

Venkata Rao explained, 'For some reason, I am fascinated and curious about such things. For a long time I wanted to write a story on conjoined twins. But I had to gather more details. In America, they would have studied these twins and done extensive research and studied the written accounts about twins, and they would have recorded their findings. I have no training in such matters. I am just a journalist. I write about what I come across here and there, adding to it a little bit out of my imagination. Now I must go. My wife will get furious otherwise.' He got on his bicycle and took off.

Chapter Nineteen

The Story Within the Story

I heard about Ganga and Yamuna fifteen years ago, in Bangalore, but ever since I wrote down their story, it has coloured my seeing. Wherever I look, I come across stories and images about twins and about doubles. This is comparable to seeing my own reflection multiplied in a maze of distorting mirrors, as in some carnivals. In the same way, multiple mirror images appear in stories about twins.

American friends too have told me stories about conjoined twins. Just this year, a friend gave me books to read on twins. As I said, I have used my wife's memories and stories as if they were my own; like me, many have unconsciously purloined material for stories from someone else. Upon hearing this, my friend said, 'Ram, have you read Wallace's story about twins?'

Another friend reminded me, 'Mark Twain wrote about Ching-Ming, the conjoined twins. Born in Siam, they found a job in an American circus company and became very famous. They were called the "Siamese Twins" and after that, all conjoined twins have been called the same. It seems that one of them became a drunkard and the other was sober and pious. Both married separately, had their own children, goods, and chattels. Over 1,000 of their descendents are still around. A research study about them is now under way.'

When Ellen Richie heard a story I told about twins, she lifted her chin to show me a scar. (My sister too had a similar scar on her chin when she tripped on a flight of stairs and cut herself. An iodine-soaked pad of cotton was placed on it and the next morning the pad, stiff with dried blood and iodine, stuck out from her chin. I teased her all day, saying, 'Sumithra has grown a beard. A beard, a beard!' She couldn't stop crying. Thinking about it after all these years I feel guilty. Now my sister is twenty-six, has three children, and lives in Ahmadabad with her husband who works in a cotton factory. I was about to tell you something else, but got sidetracked. I can't help these associations.)

When she heard the tale of twins from me, my friend's wife, Ellen Richie, said, 'Wait, why are so many of us fixated on the idea of twins? Your story jogged my memory. I want to show you something.' She lifted her face pointing to the underside of her chin, the site of a two-inch-long scar. 'I don't know for how long I had this scar or how I got it. But, for a long time I thought that it was from an operation to separate me from my twin sister, stuck at birth, right here below my chin. I believed that she died during surgery and I survived, and that my parents loved her more than they loved me. I, the unwanted one, survived by devouring my twin, and I have been haunted by this for a long time,' she said.

She is not alone in such fancies, let me tell you. There was Lina, a woman from Hawaii, who had studied with my wife. Often in her sleep she would wake up screaming from nightmares. Then she would go to church, light tall white candles and pray. She was a surviving twin. Her twin sister came out first but died at birth. She was killed by the umbilical cord twisted around her neck. Lina was born next, sideways. A difficult delivery and the mother almost died. Lina felt that she had survived because of her sister's death; she felt guilty, as if she had committed an unpardonable sin. She would ask herself, 'What have I gained or achieved by being alive?'

Martin Luther also experienced a moment of change after a similar experience: he was out walking with a friend, and a sudden bolt of lightning killed the other man. Luther was thereafter searching for an answer to his question, 'Why did I not die?' Once asked, the question transformed his view of the world. There are innumerable stories on the transforming power of surviving a catastrophic death.

If one of a pair of conjoined twins, a Ganga or a Yamuna, were to die, and the other survived, wouldn't the survivor suffer in the same way? While alive, they might have quarrelled with each other constantly, and yet after one of them dies, wouldn't the other suffer dreadful pain and guilt?

I was not sure if I should send all these pages to AKR. What if he published them as his stories? No one knows much about me, I have not published much. Even my name, K. K. Ramanujan, would become a creation of his imagination. People will think that the story about my meeting him and writing about him were the product of his imagination. Creativity can come from the demonic! It cannibalizes real people to create imagined ones. Facts become fiction, and the fictitious becomes the real. When I began writing an autobiography, I thought of writing the truth as honestly as I could. I am not sure if that is possible at all.

Are all writers like this? Ever since I started writing this autobiography, I have been trying to understand the connection between what happened and what is created with words. Anything I hear or smell, I feel compelled to put down in writing; somewhat like how I felt when I hugged a tree at age fifteen, not caring whether it was a tree or a girl. Now the impulse to write has taken over. My writing self feels heavier and heavier like the old demon riding on Sinbad's back.

A friend in college, Mari Rao, became a journalist; he also wrote stories every now and then. He very much wanted to become a writer. He told me once, 'When my father died, we were all at his bedside. As he lay dying, rolling his eyes, unable to breathe, you know what I was thinking? How can I write all this in a story? I was wondering what form I could use, what words?' He was disgusted with himself, he said.

Chapter Twenty

The House Without Pillars

I told you about going to the lawyer's office with Appa. I later learned that it was a matter concerning my Doddatthe, Appa's elder sister Alamelamma, who became a widow in 1956. Appa respected her late husband. Mr Ranganathan started working as a clerk in a British firm in 1910 or thereabout. His English employers were so pleased at his command of English that they promoted him to be the manager of the entire company by 1940. He knew all the prominent people in town. He knew the editor of *The Hindu*, the mayor of Madras, the singer M.S. Subbalaxmi, the heads of the film industry (films were becoming popular then), and some actors and actresses as well. Though he was orthodox and wore the namam like other Iyengars[†] on his forehead, once in a while he enjoyed a shot of whisky. Appa remembered going to a party with him once. A film actress tweaked Mr Ranganathan's cheek and touched his lips with her fingers, all the while giggling. Appa could not get over his surprise. Appa too admired Ranganathan's command of English, his clever conversation, his aristocratic lifestyle, his emancipation from the traditional bonds and conventions. A British woman who came to his retirement party recited a poem by Shelley. Mr Ranganathan was so affected by the recitation, that he was moved to tears for all to see. Appa said, 'Such people have artistic temperaments. He was artistic.'

But, Mr Ranganathan, my Doddappa, did not have any regard for his own wife. Maybe he thought of her as being dim-witted. They did not even speak to each other much. He did not take her out with him either. As he moved up in his social position, she became increasingly confined to a room downstairs in the house. A cook prepared food for her. When Appa went there, he would first meet her in her room downstairs, then he would go upstairs to meet his beloved Bhava,[†] and there would be no mention of Doddatthe. On that Sunday when Appa and I went to their house, Appa did not take me upstairs. So, I did not see Mr Ranganathan who had been bedridden by then. What I am telling you was gleaned by me from bits of conversation I overheard between Appa and Amma.

The trip to his house in Mylapur[†] that day was my second visit. Ten years earlier I had been there with Appa and Amma. It was a massive house, with pillars that had black and white stripes. He had three servants. Doddatthe asked the cook to serve me uppittu[†] and sugar. Their large green backyard could be seen from all the windows. A short Totapuri mango tree[†] was filled with near-ripe mangoes. I gently squeezed one of the fruits without plucking it. The fruit was half yellow, half green. I was too nervous to pluck any mangoes. When we were returning to Thiruvellikkeni in their black car, I looked at Amma, hoping to see a few mangoes Doddatthe might have given her. Finding none, I was disappointed. That day Appa was in a sombre mood. There was something seriously wrong with Mr Ranganathan.

'Who knows how long he will live. What will happen to Alamelu?' Appa said, and Amma probably said in a whisper, 'Why shouldn't we bring her to Mysore?'

Doddatthe's story was even stranger than that of Chikkatthe. She had lived with her husband, but probably never had a married life. For forty years! No one knows why things turned out that way. Some people told a story: Komala ('Komli' or 'Komu' for short) was the only daughter Ranganathan had, but she was his daughter through his first wife thirty years earlier. Ranganathan took some strangers' recommendation and had his young daughter (who had just attained her menarche) married away to a simpleton from a village, just because he, the groom, had money. This girl, who was raised in a big city couldn't live in the village for long. By the time her father rose in society, she came away to Madras and began living at home. Soon she took charge of running the house, thereby marginalizing her stepmother, my Doddatthe, even more.

More than that, within a few years, she had an affair with a man from Kerala called Kannan who had entered the household as a servant. One of his duties was to give massages to Ranganathan. Soon he became his employer's favourite and stayed on. He found favour with Komala too, and she had a baby boy. Her simpleton of a husband visited her, oh, maybe once in two months; he was so ordinary-looking and wore a towel on his shoulders, and chewed betel leaves. He played with the baby thinking that it was his own. 'He has no shame,' Amma said. Other than Doddatthe, no one spoke to him.

The entire household was controlled by Komala, her father, her lover, and her son Gopala. Alameluatthe loved the child dearly. 'Gopu, my grandson,' she would call him. Later, Kannan used Ranganathan Iyengar's money and influence to buy a film studio near Salem. I won't tell you its name. I am sure you know it. It is a famous company even now.

When Ranganathan lay on his deathbed, Komala and Kannan wouldn't let Alameluatthe upstairs to see her dying husband. I cannot say whether he wanted to see his wife. When he died, there was not even a mention of Alamelu in the will. As I said, Appa and I went to see the lawyer in 1956; I suspect that this visit was to discuss the matter of Alamelu. When his brother-in-law was still alive, Appa was careful and just whispered with the lawyer. Later, after his Bhava's[†] death, Appa went to the same lawyer, to dispatch legal notices to Komala and to meet her lawyers. He was able to get for Doddatthe an out-of-court settlement of twenty-five rupees a month annuity for life. Twenty-five rupees a month! Need I say more about the bargaining power of the rich. Since she had no one else to turn to, Doddatthe came to Mysore to live with us.

She came to live with us, but soon she took control of our own household and started reigning over us. She used her position of being a 'sister-in-law' to Amma and usurped the power she never had been allowed before. Each day she insisted that she get her bath first before the rest of us. Her baths took a whole hour. She would empty the hot water tub, taking her bath until the wood in the stove had completely burned out. Twice a week she would take an oil bath. As she applied bath oil on her body, she would spill the oil all over the bathroom. After her ablutions, and after muttering the two little lines of mantra she knew, she would mark her forehead with a dot of shree churna; then, after bowing to the icon of Lord Rama,[†] she would drink a huge pot of coffee. By then it would be nine in the morning. Then sometimes she rubbed extra oil on her fat little feet, lest they get excessively dry and cracked. She would walk all around the house on her oily feet. When the sunlight fell on the cement floors, we could see everywhere her oily footprints.

On the eleventh day of the fortnight of the new moon, she didn't eat rice. But she would demand a feast of snacks to be prepared for her: Madras kali, uttappum, idli or dosa[†]—nothing less would do. Amma had to prepare them with her own hands, as food prepared by anyone else was unacceptable to her. Amma had to grind the dough the previous night. Amma had never been bothered by her in-laws till then. Now, in her middle years, she had to take on this burden.

Amma became pregnant that year, when she was fifty (the baby died). One night she placed the soaked rice and the urad dal in the grinding stone and began grinding, making the 'gada gada gada gada' sound which woke me up. Amma's face was swollen and grim with anger.

I said, 'Amma, why do you have to do all this in your condition? Doesn't Doddatthe know that you are pregnant? She is tyrannizing you in your own house! I'll tell Appa!' I was angry.

Suddenly, Amma became calm. Perhaps she was pleased that I voiced her anger; or maybe she wanted to hide her own feelings; or worse, Doddatthe might have been in the next room; or perhaps

Amma wanted to suffer like saint Sakhubai.[†] Whatever the case, Amma said, 'Be quiet. Don't make a noise.'

When I raised my voice again in anger, she said, 'Don't tell Appa any of this. He knows! He has let it go on. To be pregnant at my age, even I am ashamed of that.'

She wiped her face and said, 'On top of it, no one has done her a good turn in all her life. Poor Doddatthe! I will do what I can, and pay back what is owed her, on behalf of all who have failed her.'

She continued grinding. The next day Doddatthe devoured ten servings of the finest of idlis, soft as jasmine.

But, later that night, Doddatthe got a severe bout of pain in her belly. We were kept awake all night from her moaning and groaning. She went to the bathroom in the backyard again and again, grumbling all the while. Amma filled an empty Horlicks bottle with hot water. She gave it to Doddamma as a hot water bottle to place against her swollen stomach. She looked after Doddatthe with great love. She said, 'Please stretch your legs and sleep straight on the bed. Don't bend your knees. Shall I prepare some ginger tea for indigestion?' That night, even in my half-sleep I heard Amma's voice filled with self-satisfaction, content with what she had done. It was wicked of me to wonder if Amma had given way to her anger and laced the idli mixture with a diarrhoea pill.

When she lived with us in Mysore, Doddatthe did not help with the housework even a little bit. But she always talked about her 'good old days' in Madras. She bragged about her Mylapur house[†]—how big the house was, how cool it remained in the summer, how she was driven in her black car to the temple.

In Mysore we used to walk to the temple near the palace on Krishna Janmashtami[†] festival days. Because she applied oil on her legs, the dust from the road would get stuck to Doddatthe's feet far more than it would on the rest of us. Like a cat trying to wipe off its feet after dipping in a puddle of water, Doddatthe would carefully kick her heels to clean them.

Once we hired a horse-drawn carriage to go to the temple. Appa sat in the back, facing the road along with Amma and Tangi,[†] and I sat with Doddatthe behind the horse. The horse must have been fed too much horse-gram that day and was flatulent. All along the road it kept breaking wind, 'brurr…brurr...brurr….' Like a pair of bellows blowing hot air, the horse pumped gas directly into Doddatthe's face. Amma made signs to Tangi and me not to laugh, but she herself could hardly contain her grin. Appa's face tightened in an angry knot. From that day, Doddatthe never rode in a horse-drawn carriage. She probably thought about her black car in Madras a great deal that day.

Whenever Doddatthe spoke of her luxurious past in Madras, Amma's face flamed in anger. 'Her husband didn't even look at her, even for one day. Now I burn in anger when I hear her vain tales of her Mylapur black car, her huge home, her mango-chutney, this, that, tuss…puss…, and what else. I know it is just the sound of an empty pot rattling. Even when it grates on me, I feel sorry for her,' Amma said.

One day, Doddatthe began grumbling, as if she had nothing better to do. Wouldn't it be nice to have a teak swing between a pair of black pillars right here in the middle of the main room? In her Mylapur home she had just such pillars, four of them in the main room. 'Gopala, my grandson' ran around the pillars. Each month servants polished the pillars with oil to perfection. Doddatthe said, 'You could see your reflection as in a mirror.' First, Amma got angry, but then she pitied the old woman.

Two or three days later Doddatthe sat on a bench on the verandah, rolled her eyes and stared into space, daydreaming. She was probably seeing her non-existent black pillars and the teak swing between them, and listening to the clicks and creaks of imaginary chains and pulleys, when I almost burst out laughing. Then, as I noticed the direction of her gaze, I too began to see black pillars and a teak swing shining right there in the middle of the hall but I snapped out of it soon and said, 'Doddatthe, are you seeing your Madras pillars and swing here?

Shall I tell you a trick: If you make a diagram on your eyeglasses, with no cost to you at all you will have built a pair of pillars and a swing. I will ask Appa to do the same, if you want!'

She made a face saying, 'You are always making fun of me. Get away. Mind your own business.'

Yet, I couldn't get over the illusion of the pillars inside one's eyes. A pair of pillars with no home.

The same week an unknown man showed up to see Doddatthe. He could have been a driver of some sort. He spoke in half-Kannada, half-Tamil and said, 'I wish to see Doddatthe.' Like film stars, he wore a pair of dark glasses, kept a thin mustache, a checkered handkerchief around his neck under the collar of his sport shirt, and he had a dark, lightly powdered face. Perhaps, before getting a role as an actor in a movie, you must work as a driver for the film stars. Or it could be that proximity would influence your gestures. Whatever it was, his strange theatrical style was aimed at a camera eye. He came in with no hesitation, did not even remove his shoes, did not salute Doddatthe, and sat down on a chair. I was quite upset; neither Amma nor Doddatthe allowed anyone to come into the house without removing their shoes, saying, 'Who knows what they stepped on', but that man had walked into the house with his shoes on. Instead, Doddatthe just gave me a dignified gentle look, saying, 'Gopala, my grandson, has sent a personal message from Madras; he wants to speak to me.'

She waved her hands as if to dispose of me. I even had to bring coffee for the bounder. He raised the silver cup to his lips, took a casual sip as if he were an aristocrat, and did not even finish all of the coffee.

From that Monday through the rest of the week, Doddatthe remained highly excited. Her grandson had sent her a message that he would come and see her on Saturday.

'He is coming in connection with some film company work; he is very young, only twenty-four. Soon he will own the entire company. He always calls me "Paati, Paati" (meaning "Grandma, Grandma"), said Doddatthe.

Then she said to me, 'Be at your best. Wear good clothes. You are a good boy.'

She went to Amma advising her about what food to serve, 'I am not sure if he will eat here or not. But prepare some nice snacks for him. He loves cashew halva and dumrote,[†] but he does not use buffalo milk in his coffee.' Doddatthe fussed about all the details. We were curious, but not too pleased. 'Let us see about this man. Let him show up,' was how we thought about it. We all knew Doddatthe's grandson's history.

Amma said, 'What has happened to this woman! All these days she fussed about her Mylapur house, the pillars, the swing, the mango trees, her black car, and the pot of gold in the mirror; now, all she can think of is her grandson's grand parade! That grandson probably didn't even look at her, or even speak to her a single time. Now she treats him as if he were a prince! Come to think of it, he may not be really her grandson. His mother Komala did not spend even one night with her husband.'

But, as Friday and Saturday came, Amma spent all day in the kitchen, spent hours grumbling and cooking cashew halva, dumrote, and sesame seed fried snacks. She even bought cow's milk for coffee for our royal visitor.

I don't think Doddatthe slept well the night before her grandson's expected arrival. She went to the bathroom two or three times, made enough noise cleaning herself and didn't let us sleep in peace. Soon after she woke up in the morning, she massaged her legs and feet with oil. She oiled her twelve strands of hair with coconut oil; normally she would do this only before going to the temple. She wore her white silk sari with the red border.

Although Doddatthe normally looked like a baby elephant, on that day her face had the glow of maize. There was a rare gaiety in her demeanour and a spring to her gait.

Her grandson had not told her at what hour to expect him, or told her how many guests he would bring with him. This worried

Amma. If dozens of people from his film industry showed up, how could she manage? She told the milkmaid, 'If I need more milk, I'll send word. Keep some extra for me, just in case.'

By the time the clock struck noon, we were all restless. Venku went to see a movie. I stayed home and tasted the cashew halva. 'Why can't you wait for one more minute?' Doddatthe said in an angry voice. Are we, mere mortals, not supposed to eat anything until Lord Gopala is served, I thought.

She went near the door five times in ten minutes, thinking her grandson was there. She asked me to walk up to the end of the street, as far as the Hundred Foot Road and see if he was coming.

'Here comes a carriage,' I shouted seeing a horse-driven vehicle. Doddatthe said, 'He will never hire a horse carriage! Look for a taxi or a car!' She was right. Five minutes later, the carriage arrived and went past our house sounding its bells from the horse's chain; Gopala was not there. Instead I saw it held an extremely obese woman with a large kumkum; her weight was enough to make the carriage sag to the ground. She went to the third house from ours.

Appa came downstairs and told Doddatthe, 'Some hanger-on comes along and tells you some nonsense and you trust him. Alamelu, you have been like this all your life, ever since your childhood. How naive you are! Those rotten loafers from the studios! Who knows where they are loitering now!' He roared, he grumbled, he ate the dumrote Amma had made, and went back upstairs to his study.

By six in the evening, Appa got really cross. He picked up his jacket, his scarf, and the walking stick, came down from his office, and went to the market for shopping. Amma said, 'Keep the door open. It is twilight; the hour of the Goddess Laxmi.' Then, as she did each Saturday, Amma made the servants give the jasmine, the roses, and sugandharaja plants their usual drink of water and the servants used brooms to sweep the front yard and around the gate. Then she sprinkled the yard with water, and using the decorative rangoli† powder, she drew a lotus with eight petals. She came in, lighted a lamp oiled with ghee, placed it in front of the household god, offered evening prayers, and went back to cook.

Doddatthe's disappointment on that day depressed all of us. Although Gopala had sent word of his arrival in Mysore, no one knew where he was staying, or for what sort of work he had come there. I went to my neighbour's house, borrowed the evening paper, *Saadhwi* and looked to see if any of his movies were running in nearby theaters. In fact, in Ukkada, on the outskirts of town, there was a movie running in Kalindi Talkies[†] that fit the description. I felt like running home and telling Doddatthe about it, and even taking her to the Kalindi Talkies so that she might see her beloved grandson. My urge to do this was quite intense.

That Saturday, Doddatthe's 'grandson' (who was really not her grandson) never showed up. He did not even send word as to his whereabouts. I was angry, sad, disgusted, disappointed, and wrung out with emotions. I went through what Amma experienced over Doddatthe: first the anger, then the attempts to suppress anger, and in the end, a pervasive sadness.

A few months after this, Doddatthe said, 'I cannot stand the December cold of Mysore. At my age I need a Vishnu temple much closer. At least I have a sister and sister-in-law in Madras.' She kept grumbling till Appa bought her a ticket to Madras, and she left Mysore for good. Amma initially thought that her departure, under a cloud, was an insult to our relationship. Amma felt sad too. She said, 'Who will look after her over there? Here, I could have made idlis for her on the eleventh and twelfth day of the new moon. This is Doddatthe's karma.' I could also see that Amma was relieved to be rid of the unnecessary conflicts, and the extra work.

Chapter Twenty-one

Red Oxen in Chicago

Doddatthe suffered much in her Mylapur house, but once she came to Mysore and began living with us, she seemed to miss her old house and kept up a babble about the four pillars, the teak swings, and her grandson. Ambivalence sometimes passes for 'home sickness' or 'nostalgia', and Doddatthe's obsessive talk was seen as a longing to return 'home'.

I received a response from Chicago. AKR wrote, 'This is nothing out of the ordinary. A desire to get back home, or to return to one's birthplace, is most common. As Tukaram and other great saints have said, this world is the in-law's place; the soul longs to return to the mother's place.' Nowadays AKR is overdoing it, with his long tales and harikathas.[†] He even included a poem.

> Have I not said
> If born in Talkadu[†]
> Your mind will
> Continue to drown
> In jungle waterholes
> Or in snowy Switzerland
> Don't dream of dosas
> At wedding receptions
> In America
> Do not expect
> Pan or kumkum.

Homesickness remains in the blood of expatriates like us in foreign lands. There is no cure. Even if you go back home, the malaise continues. The home you go to is different from the one you left. If you were to order a fruit salad, don't expect it to be the fruit salad you ate with your father twenty years ago. There could be temporary relief. A Hindi writer from Udaipur,[†] a well-known poet, came to Chicago. He visited my Iowa friends in May. I arranged for a group to hear him give a performance of his poems.

Being a Rajasthani,[†] he sported a large mustache. He wore sandals and silk kurtas over a dhoti. He was about fifty years old, and had wide-set eyes and a broad nose. He was tall, lean, and handsome, and sure to attract a second glance. His keen eyes made him look like a Rajput warrior[†] looking for his lost horse. Later, I learned that his horizon-scanning gaze was due to his poor eyesight, for I noticed that when reading, he held the page at a noticeable distance.

Though he had travelled all over the world, at heart he was the same as when he lived in his village. On one of the two days that he stayed in Iowa, I came upon him as he was eating lunch in an office. He was alone there, yet he was crouching behind a desk as if to avoid being observed while he ate.

He was in fact very smart. He wrote poems in a Rajasthani dialect, daring the nationalistic Hindi poets. He used to say that we must look not just at Hindi, but dozens of other dialects, such as Avadhi, Maithili.[†] He said that we mustn't 'recite' poetry but sing it. He was an English teacher, but his research was on folklore and folksongs.

He had already spent two of his six months in this country. He said that the first two months here were the worst for him. He stayed at the International House on 59th Street in Chicago. For a month he had not received a letter from his wife. He did not like the food at the cafeteria. He didn't relish the bread, the insipid peas soaked in water, corn on the cobs. He couldn't find his favourite areca nuts, but managed to get some from an Italian grocery store. The store even had fenugreek, papad, green dal, Bedekar pickles, hot green chillis, curry leaves, and cilantro. The store-owner told him that if he could, he would import betel leaves by air. When Prasad asked the Italian hesitatingly, if he had areca nuts, the man showed off his Hindi and said, 'Supari, supari', and gave him all he needed. Prasad bought a pound of supari. Using the nutcracker he had brought from Rajasthan, he pealed the areca nuts, layer by layer and began chewing them. Even though he had no betel leaves, he chewed the dry areca nuts to great satisfaction. I saw him holding his nutcracker. I can't be sure if it was made of copper or bronze. The two blades were in the shape of a male and female figure, like Radha and Krishna. When opened, the two figures stayed apart. When the nuts were inserted and cracked, the figures joined each other as if they were doing it. Prasad's Khajuraho[†] nutcracker.

No one spoke his language here. Some spoke Hindi and Punjabi.[†] Prasad visited them, ate paratha and gulab jamun,[†] spoke about India, and became even more homesick. He longed to see his wife and children. All day he felt empty, uneasy, and confused. He spent five to six hours in the library but could not write much. By then it was November.

One evening, a white blanket of the first heavy snowfall covered the gutters, the roofs, the parked cars. He saw black leafless trees sticking up like black marks, and the trashcans all covered in white. He saw no acute angles anywhere; all the corners were blurred in a white softness. Seeing a landscape so beautiful in a strange foreign land, he felt as if a whispering silence was spreading all over, and that the whole world was moving towards silence. It continued to snow at night, a powdery snow, white and woolly, as if the whole sky was two miles nearer than ever before, like placing a white cap on the expanse of the universe.

If his mind had been blocked earlier, now he was distraught. He wanted to get out of his room, but he couldn't run far in the snow. Still, he went outside hurriedly, without his winter coat. He dipped his hands into the foot-high snow piled on top of a parked car; he grabbed a handful and mashed the snow into his face, neck, chest and inside his unbuttoned shirt, as if to take in the cold white snow into himself. It was already one in the morning. There was no one around. After five minutes of this madness, he came to, and although he was shivering in the wintry air, he was pleased that he could feel his body's heat responding to the frosty snow. He felt a new excitement after his first snow.

This was only a temporary relief from his despair. The snow started melting, men trudged over it, cars ran over it and the black soot from Chicago factories soiled it. The street was now a long half-white and dirty-black puddle. His momentary happiness too melted away.

Homesickness tends to relapse unexpectedly. Many years ago, a friend of mine in college went to Kerala as a teacher after his BA honours, to a town called Changanacheri, a typical Malayali town. Great food. Great bananas. Great people. He even learned a bit of Malayalam. The girls were well built and strong; they were graceful. He was generally a hail-fellow-well-met man. One day as he turned into a small street, he heard a gramophone playing a Kannada film song. Unable to control himself, he sobbed. Telling this to us when he came back to Mysore, he laughed at himself.

Recently, an American youngster who joined the Peace Corps landed in a village in the middle of Andhra. He learned Telugu[†] and lived among the farmers for nine months, eating like them, working like them, talking like them. One day he went to Vishakhapattanam to see a girl from America. It was the first time in a year he had met another American. He took her to see *Gone with the Wind*, the four-hour American civil war saga. As he sat in the movie theatre, his memories rushed back: the smell of his American home, his mother, father. Suddenly he lost control of his usual well-bred ways. His whole life came back to him; his emotions took hold of him and he began shouting in the theatre. Someone asked him to be quiet. He became infuriated and started beating up the man; the girl who was with him did not know what to do. She begged him to stop, and kept repeating, 'Michael! Michael!' Then, some hooligans attacked him and the police came and took him to a mental hospital. Prasad himself told me all this.

He also told me the case of another Hindi-speaking man he knew in Chicago. The man told Prasad that every day on waking he would invariably think about his home; then he would feel depressed and empty; by afternoon he would have recovered. For weeks he wondered why it was like this. One day, as he was brushing his teeth and tasting the toothpaste, he became more and more anxious, and then he had a revelation. The man's wife had packed ten tubes of Neem toothpaste in his suitcase, saying, 'You can't find these in America. Your Neem toothpaste; take them.'

The man said that his family had always used Neem toothpaste; he had been accustomed to the pleasant bitter taste of Neem leaves from when he was ten years old, and that he associated it with home. Now he realized that Neem toothpaste was responsible for stirring up his subconscious, bringing back his memory of home, and in its wake, feelings of depression and emptiness. That day, he threw away the remaining tubes of toothpaste, and bought an American brand. The man told Prasad that since then, he had found it easier to accept his life in America.

Prasad too was unhappy. He got addicted to areca nuts; chewing them brought him some comfort. But his mind found no relief. He felt like ending his trip and going back home. Then he remembered a long story he had heard in a Rajasthani village. For several years he had meant to write the story. He normally didn't write prose, he was a poet. But now he felt that writing a story would be a good remedy for his insomnia. When he came to Iowa, he narrated to me the story he had written.

Kharigaum, he said, was an ordinary simple Rajasthani village of about five hundred people. It was in a desert region, but there was a small river and a pond, and therefore, at least for about six months each year, the village remained green. It was actually a very charming peaceful village.

An old man came to Kharigaum once, in search of his lost ox that had a single horn. He said that the ox was the sum total of his life's possession. With it he could plough and earn a little bit of money. He appeared lost and demented as he went about looking for the ox with the single horn. The villagers didn't know who he was. He slept in an old temple outside the village, but they didn't let him stay there in peace even for a few days. Some said he was one of the dacoits, that he was there to check out their village for the purpose of plundering and looting. Some said that he worked as a government agent for the CID,[†] the Criminal Investigation Department. Some thought he was an escaped convict. Even young boys in the village heard the rumours and started harassing him.

The old man went around looking for his lost ox in the jungles around the village. He would bring rice and bread from somewhere and cook his meal using bits of firewood in a tandoor oven he had built from wayside bricks and stones. One day, some street boys hid nearby and threw pebbles at him. They brought a box containing head lice and dropped them on his bed. They tore and burned the dhotis he had spread out for drying. Finally one day, they placed a large frog and a red scorpion on his bed. He felt scared when he looked up and saw the urchins taunting him as they fled. The next day he went away.

A week later a middle-aged woman came there looking for him. She brought two uniformed servants with her. She was not wearing a veil. One could tell that she was well educated. From the looks of her servants and her dignified demeanour, she must have been royalty. People went out of their way to please her. She had the entire village assembled around the verandah of a local rich man, and for six hours she interrogated each of the villagers about that old man and the ox with one horn. Her servants went about checking the horns of the oxen in the village. She left the next day.

In the same village, a college student, on vacation, felt bad for the old man. He believed that the old man was not a dacoit, nor an undercover CID agent; he was just a simple unhappy old man who had lost his ox. The student said that as a matter of fact, it happened to be true: the old man had lost his single-horned ox, and that the villagers had been unfair to him. The urchin pranksters had been cruel. As the college student began arguing about the old man with the head of the village on a hot afternoon on the outskirts of the village, he saw from the corner of his eyes, a man chasing something past the shrubbery and raising dust. He told the headman to wait for a second and he ran after the man.

Someone was indeed running on that dusty road. His dhoti was flying around him as he ran; he was almost a mile away. It was the same old man. His shirt was soiled, his hair dishevelled, and his graying beard unkempt. The old man didn't stop, even after hearing the student shouting, 'Hey, stop! Stop, old man! Don't run! I won't harm you. Please stop!' The old man got scared when he noticed that the student was chasing him. He began to run even faster to get away. His old ox must have been feeling the same as it tried to escape. Soon the old man grew tired. Unable to continue any further, he sat near a rock by the roadside, trying to catch his breath. The student was right behind him. The old man looked pathetic; he was tired, hungry, and scared; he was breathless; he was drooling.

'Why do you harass me like this?' he said, still trying to catch his breath. He was speaking in his Rajasthani village dialect, and he looked as if he was about to weep. The young man spoke to him in a gentle voice.

'Please don't misunderstand. I want to talk to you. That is why I ran after you. Our village has done you harm. Aren't you searching for your one-horned ox?' he said.

'Yes, I was about to find it. Just then the boys of your village burned my clothes, dropped a scorpion on my bed, and drove me away,' the old man said.

'Uncouth rascals! What can we do about such ignorant people! Forget them; don't worry about them. Have you found your ox?'

'I have not seen it for days. I have roamed through many villages. On the day I first came here, I saw it around your village, and again I saw it today.'

'Where did you see it?'

'There, right over there, my rogue of a red ox disappeared into dust. It is not a fully trained ox, and it does not know its whereabouts. So I spanked it a few times, and it ran away again. I was chasing it, when I heard you behind me. I got scared and kept running.'

'Which way did your ox run? Tell me. Was he running away from you, escaping from you?'

The old man looked up at that moment, and with a gleam in his eyes, he said with great conviction, 'No, no, he didn't mislead me. There! Can you see over there? There's my red ox!' He pointed at the hill on the other side of the small creek in which the water seemed still.

'Where? On the hill over there?'

'Right there, sir! Can't you see its single horn? Look at the bulge on its back.' With his finger he drew the outlines of the hill in the red dust. On the left corner, there was a solitary, leafless tree, sticking up like an ox's horn. A huge boulder bulged over the back of the hill and it looked like a bull as large as a thousand feet, ribcage and all, as if an unknown artist had fashioned it. Backlit by the evening sun already sinking beyond the hill, a huge dark bull appeared like a giant shadow against the sky. The college student kept staring at it. Against the outline, the tree on top of the hill appeared to be a single horn. As he stared at it, he saw the mouth of the ox, its nose, and profile. The reflection of this 'bull' floated upside down on the surface of the still creek.

'See, how it is sleeping now!' said the old man, pointing to the reflection. 'I must go and catch it, must rope and get it to my place,' the old man said, springing up.

Shankara Prasad had written this story only thus far. A friend of mine said, as in other Hindi stories of that generation, the college student in his story must have been Prasad himself.

He took about six to eight days to write this story. He wrote it on legal-sized white sheets, crossed out much of it and rewrote. There were about twenty-five pages about the village, the people, the folklore and whatnot. (I have left out the details here.) On the top right border of each sheet, he noted the page number in Hindi script. During Chicago's midwinter, he sat in his room on the sixth floor of the International House, and managed to visualize the dust motes in his Rajasthani village; he could feel the burning desert sun, and he continued to work on the story day after day.

For many years he had narrated the same story to his wife and friends, so much so, its characters and descriptions had been talking to him all along. Only the unwritten stories haunt us; they talk to us and stay with us. Once it is written, it is laid to rest. Those who had heard him tell the story asked him to write it down. Now 10,000 miles away, alone, with not a single person to read what he wrote, he was able to set it down on paper. On the eighth floor, there were two engineering students who could read Hindi, but he didn't feel like showing it to them. In mid-December in snow-laden Chicago, his story came to life.

That Sunday evening, some Indian students had invited Prasad to a party some thirty-five miles away in Winnetka. A government officer from Delhi, who had been transferred to Washington, was visiting his doctor brother's house for a couple of days. He had heard of Shankara Prasad's poetry, and since he knew some twenty others who spoke Hindi, the bureaucrat from Delhi had assembled a group to hear Shankara Prasad recite his poems. The listeners were moved by Prasad's lyrical Rajasthani poems. But as soon as the reading ended, they moved on to listen to Hindi film songs on a cassette player.

Prasad felt uncomfortable. In the kitchen, there was a sixteen-year-old cook. The women were helping him, as the boy prepared the dinner. He had been brought over from India as a cook for the home of the bureaucrat. He knew no English, but spoke in a perfect Rajasthani dialect. The lad was from a village near Jaipur; he was thrilled to hear Prasad sing Rajasthani poems. Prasad found out that the boy's father received two hundred rupees for his son's service in the kitchen of the bureaucrat.

Prasad felt sad: he too had once been a boy from a village in

Rajasthan; while in school, he had not shown any interest in his studies. An uncle on his mother's side had even been to jail. Arrested in Prasad's home, the uncle was taken to Udaipur in handcuffs. Prasad had spent his childhood surrounded by people who could provide little.

But on the other side, his father's elder brother had been a chef, and this uncle wanted to start a restaurant. One day he came to the village and said to Prasad's father, 'Send your son with me. I will teach him how to cook One of these days he will find a job.'

He took twelve-year-old Prasad with him to Udaipur. There, the uncle's situation improved; he bought a restaurant, and somehow out of an unexpected generous impulse, he told Prasad one day, 'Stop working in the kitchen. Enough of cooking lessons for now. Look after the cash register.' The uncle enrolled him in a school. Prasad worked part-time at the restaurant and eventually managed to go to a college. To this day, he doesn't know how to cook.

Prasad thought, 'There's but a hair's breadth dividing me from that boy. Like him, I too would have been in a kitchen making rotis[†] and stirring soup. I wouldn't be reciting poems in a room filled with listeners; I would have been listening to the poetry recital, standing in the kitchen. I could have been that boy in the kitchen, but for my uncle's generous impulse.'

By midnight, they had sung film songs and thumris,[†] played the tabla,[†] and told old jokes. It was time for him to say goodbye to his friends and his host. He thought of meeting that boy in the kitchen, speaking to him in Rajasthani dialect and patting him on his back. In the kitchen, the boy had put away the leftover rotis, soups, and sweets in the refrigerator. He had done the dishes, spread a long towel in the corner, and had gone to sleep on the floor, as servants do in India. He probably had a different place to sleep, but as was his old habit, he might have felt like sleeping on the floor of the kitchen.

By the time Prasad reached the International House, it was already one in the morning. He got in, and without even removing his jacket, started reading the story he had written.

He thought that he had never read a piece worse than what he had written; he found twisted, limping sentences, and misbegotten errors. The dialogue was stilted. He thought the story was unbelievably bad. Should he put his name to such trash! He felt disgusted. He could not read even a sentence beyond the first six or seven pages. He felt angry with himself.

He stretched his leg, moved the waste basket closer with his foot, and slowly but steadily tore up page after page, the twenty-five pages he had written. Again and again he shredded them. He tore each page into halves, and then into quarters, and the story was ripped into small pieces. Soon, he had hundreds of tiny squares too small to tear any further. He dumped them in the wastebasket. Hundreds of systematically fractured sentences, tiny square bits bearing letters, were now a pile of confetti in the wastebasket.

He got up and walked to the bathroom at the end of the corridor, took a piss, cleaned and rinsed his mouth; he got back to his room, changed into his T-shirt and knickers. He lay on his bed, stretched his body, turned off the lamp, and tried to get some sleep. The radium dial of his Tokyo-made wristwatch glowed green, its numbers and arms pointing to two-thirty in the morning.

He was tired. He could not sleep. He got up to drink some water. He opened the window to let in some fresh air. Unable to sleep, he once again put on his pyjamas, went out to the toilet, came back and tried to sleep. Now the hands of his watch pointed to three. The next-door neighbour's radio too had ended its piano programme.

'Why did I come this far, to this country? I should go back tomorrow!' he thought. He could feel the pounding in his head.

Suddenly he got up, turned on the lights, dressed again, this time with a shirt and a jacket, stepped into his Rajasthani sandals, picked up the wastebasket containing thousands of pieces of shredded paper. He said to himself, 'I cannot be in the same room with this anymore.'

He opened the door. He walked in his noisy sandals through the desolate, dim-lit corridor. On the other side of the water fountain, inside the bathroom there was a large dustbin, man-sized, standing silently. It was filled with the day's trash: paper plates, cigarette butts, stinking ashtrays, and flattened empty toothpaste tubes. There was an American-made yellow condom that looked like a blown out, spit-filled balloon, flat and wet. In this so-called men's hostel, how did this get here, he wondered. Looking up, he forgot his own question. In the bathroom mirror he saw his own messy face—red eyes, sparse unkempt strands on the crown of his large shining brown dome of a head; and he could see his outstretched hands holding a wastebasket away from his body, like those sewage-cleaners holding buckets of dung. 'Hell! At three in the morning, everything appears metaphorical,' he grumbled to himself.

He turned the wastebasket upside down into that big drum. The torn pieces of his story fell into the drum. Looking inside the wastebasket he found one square piece of the paper sticking to a wad of white chewing gum. In spite of the disgust he felt, he picked up the gum and the piece of paper and threw them into the drum. Just before discarding it, he peered at what was written on the paper. On one side the letters read 'parasaa' and on the other side 'thoo'.

Because he had touched the gum, he washed his hands again; he studied himself in the mirror. He noticed his birthmarks, and the blue shadow to be shaved the next day. He carried his wastebasket down the dismal corridor, past each of the eleven doors, past the corner and into the half-open door of Room 676. He slipped out of his sandals, threw his shirt, jacket, and pants on a chair, turned off the lights, quietly lay down on his warm bed, and pulled the wool blanket over himself. He closed his eyes, and within a minute, even before he knew it, the comfort of sleep overtook him.

Chapter Twenty-two

Atthimber's Last Wish

During our three-day visit, I did not go back again to my Chikkatthe's house. Appa visited her twice more. The first time Atthimber managed to sit up and speak for about half an hour; he asked after each of us. He wanted a newspaper. He folded the sheets of newsprint and tore them into neat squares, and like a child, made paper boats, canoes, sailboats, a cup to hold turmeric or tilak powder, and even a sharp-beaked bird with open wings. He gave the paper bird to Appa. Atthimber's voice was weak; he said, 'Give it to Ramu. When he came here last time, I didn't even have strength to speak with him.'

Appa carefully removed from his pocket, the sharp-beaked paper bird that was made from the matrimonial pages of *The Hindu*.[†]

'He was like that. Always interested in doing handiwork. In spite of his talents, he did not achieve much in his life. He retired as a clerk at the post office,' Appa said.

I examined the paper bird trying to see how Atthimber had made it. Since he had torn the paper with a trembling hand, the edges were ragged, not sharp. Yet, for a second I could see his clever hands creating shadow plays, and I remembered the sharp-beaked bird, as if the same stork had now opened its wings. I moved it around and unfolded it completely; and it was just a square of paper with creases. No matter how much I tried, I couldn't fold it back into a bird. I stared at the matrimonial page from *The Hindu* in my hand.

That Sunday afternoon Appa made his final visit to Atthe's house. It seems that the doctor was there. The doctor said to Appa, 'This may last two more days. His swollen belly will not go down.'

Atthimber had been experiencing difficulty in eating anything for more than a month, but at that very moment when Appa was there, he heard a street hawker yelling out, 'Dried dates!' Atthimber felt a great urge to eat them. He made gestures to indicate that he wanted to eat the dry fruit, but his voice was indistinct. There was a gurgling in his throat. Atthe looked at him with love and said, 'Dates are bad for your health. Dates! They look like flattened cockroaches! Don't act like a child and ask for this and that.'

When Appa told me all this, I said, 'Why didn't you tell Atthe to go ahead and buy the dates for him?' Appa said, 'I dared not tell her what the doctor said. I just could not bring myself to say to her, 'Atthimbeeru is dying, give him whatever he wants and make him happy.' Unless I repeated the doctor's words, I knew she would not have bought any dates for him. But, had I told her, she would have felt miserable giving him dates. If she thought that she was the one feeding him his last bite here on earth, how could she bear to feed him his last meal at such a moment? No, that wouldn't have been easy for her. So I kept quiet.'

Then Appa said, 'Tonight we have to go back to Mysore. My vacation is over.' Until that very moment, I had no idea that my Appa was capable of such an intuitive and complex understanding of what was involved in responding to a dying man's wish for dried dates.

In the train that night Appa spoke of Atthimber again. 'Even prisoners on death row get to eat whatever they wish for their final meal. All sorts of snacks, sweets, and desserts. They serve them a grand meal. Poor Atthimbeeru did not even get to eat what he asked for, not even a single dried date for his last meal.'

1976–7   Northfield, Minnesota

Glossary of words

Acharya: A pundit, or a teacher.

Agni: God of fire.

Ahmadabad: A city in Gujarat.

Akka: Elder sister.

Alvars: Devotees of Vishnu, saints who wrote hymns addressed to Vishnu; AD 700–900. *See* Ramanujan's translation and introduction in *Hymns for the Drowning* (Princeton, 1981).

Ambarisha: Pious legendary king, exemplary devotee of Vishnu in the Vedas.

Anna: Elder brother.

Annas: Coins used in olden days.

Arakalagoodu: A town in Karnataka.

Ashadabhuti: Derogatory description of someone who is deceitful, yet has an appearance of being honest and congenial.

Atma: The soul.

Atthe: Aunt.

Atthige: Sister-in-law.

Avadhi, Maithili: Dialects of Hindi, spoken in Avadh and Mithila regions respectively.

Ayyo: Expression of despair and exacerbation, as in 'Oh, my god!'

Badami halwa: A Sweet with almonds.

Bala Saraswathi: Classical south Indian dancer.

Bangalore: Capital city of Karnataka state in south India.

Banni Mantap: Trees, grove of *Acacia Ferruginea*.

Basava, *Kumaravyasa*, *Kuvempu*, *Bendre*: Well-known poets who wrote in Kannada.

Belgaum: A city in Karnataka.

Bhagavadgita: Section in the Mahabharata where Lord Krishna advises the warrior prince Arjuna on the virtues of fulfilling one's duties.

Bhava: Husband's brother or sister's husband.

Bibhatsa: The muse of disgust, one of the muses in literature.

Brahmachari: An ascetic, a celibate, a student of the Vedas.

Brahmarandhra: Yogic term; door to pure consciousness, the tenth door, the central pore of the palate. The other doors are the nine orifices (eyes, ears, nostrils, mouth, anus, genital), which are open to the outside world. When these nine orifices are closed through yogic exercises, the practitioner can only perceive through the tenth door, or the Brahmadwara, or the door to pure consciousness.

Cardamom-laced betel leaves: Betel leaves with lime and cardamom, known as pan, a chewing quid.

Champa flower: Fragrant flower native to India and south-east Asia, also known as *Plumeria rubra*, *Frangipani*, *Pagoda tree*, *Temple tree*.

Chamundi Hill-shaped: In the shape of a hill near Mysore city.

Chettiyar shop: Owned by Chettiyar, a merchant class.

Chikkatthe: Younger/youngest aunt.

CID: Criminal Investigation Department.

Chiroti: A sweet.

Chitragupta: Servant and bookkeeper for Yama, Hindu god of death.

Closepet: A suburb of Bangalore.

Coimbatore: City in Tamil Nadu.

Crores: Ten million, 10,000,000.

Dussehra parades: Parade culminating the nine-day festival of Navaraatri celebrating the destruction of a demon by the gods.

Devara Dasimayya: A singing saint from the twelfth century.

Devva: Ghost, demon.

Dharwar: City in north-west Karnataka.

Dhoti: Men's sarong-like garment worn from the waist down.

Dhud, dhud, dhadak: Sound, as in dub-a-lub-a-dub.

Doddamma: Elder/eldest sister; mother's older sister.

Dosa: Pancake of rice and lentils.

Dwaraka: City of Lord Krishna; play on dwara or door (Sanskrit).

Finley dhoti: Saronglike wrap for men, manufactured by Finley company.

Ganapathy: Elephant-headed Hindu god.

Ganda berunda twin-birds: Mythical bird whith two heads and one body.

Georgetown: Former British settlement, now an extension of Madras.

Goddess Laxmi: Goddess of wealth and prosperity and Vishnu's consort.

Gopuram tower: The cupola on a temple.

Grihastha: A householder.

Gulab jamuna: Sweet.

Ha Priya Prashantha Hrudaya: First line of song from a film, 'Oh my darling, you of calm disposition'.

Halva, dumrote: Sweet dishes.

Harikathas: Literally stories of Vishnu, but these are oral performances of Puranic narratives.

Hraam hreem mantra: Refers to the mumbo-jumbo of the sorcerer.

Hyderabad: The capital city of Andhra Pradesh.

Iyengar Brahmin: South Indian Brahmin; orthodox Iyengar Brahmins wear one, two, or three vertical lines over their forehead.

Iyengars: Brahmin followers of Vishnu.

Juttu: A pony tail or queue.

Kabuli: Person from Kabul, Afghanistan.

Kali temple: Kali is the goddess of death/healing/illness.

Kalindi Talkies: A movie theatre.

Kama: Hindu god of love, Eros.

Kama's bow: Bow and arrow made of flowers of the god of love.

Kanaka: A sudra saint and bhakti poet from Udipi. According to legend,

Brahmin priests at the Udipi Krishna temple refused entry to Kanaka. Krishna heard his plea and breaking the walls of the temple showed himself to Kanaka. That hole in the wall is known as Kanakana Kindi or Kanaka's opening.

Kanakambra: Flower, indigenous to India, *Crosandra infundibuliformis*.

Kannada: The language of Karnataka, south India.

Karnataka: South Indian state.

Kavala: Slang for food, grub.

Kerala: A south Indian state.

Khajuraho: Ancient Hindu temple famous for erotic scultpure.

Koka Shastra: Ancient Hindu sex manual.

Kollegala sari: Women's wear manufactured in Kollegala, Mysore.

Kolyinos Toothpaste: A brand of toothpaste.

Krishna Janmashtami: Birthday of Lord Krishna, a religious festival.

Krishna nee begane baro: The first line of a song composed by the sage Purandhara Dasa in the sixteenth century, meaning, *Come at once, dear Lord Krishna*.

Kumkum: Red mark worn by Indian women in the middle of their forehead.

Kuppu: A name.

Lord Hanuman: King of the monkeys in the epic, Ramayana.

Lord Krishna: God, eighth incarnation of Vishnu.

Lord of Thirupathi: God Venkatesh, in Thirupathi.

Lord Rama: Hero of Ramayana, incarnation of Vishnu.

Lord Vishnu: God, protector of the universe.

Madhurai, a city in Tamil Nadu.

Madras kali, *uttappum*, *idli or dosa*: Popular south Indian dishes.

Madras: Capital of the state of Tamil Nadu, south India, now renamed Chennai.

Maharastrian ghati saris: Folk saris worn by ghati women in Maharastra.

Malayali: One who speaks the language, Malayalam, or from Malayala region (now Kerala state).

Malleswaram: A suburb in Bangalore.

Mambalam: Place in Madras.

Mangalsutra: Traditional wedding chain worn by women.

Masala vada: Fried Indian savoury cake, made with rice and lentils.

Mountain-nelli: A sour berry used in making pickles.

Muttaide: Married woman whose husband in still alive.

Mylapor house: House in a suburb of Madras (now Chennai).

Mylapur: A suburb in Madras.

Mysore: A city in Karnataka.

Namam: Traditional vertical mark worn by Iyengar Brahmins.

Navaratri: Dussehra, Hindu festival, nine nights and ten days in October.

Neem leaves: From medicinal plant, *azadirachta indica*.

Nehru shirt: Traditional Indian jacket for men, popularized by Jawaharlal Nehru.

Nishadabad: A suburb of Mysore city.

North-Karnataka speech: Dialect from north Karnataka.

Nungumbakkum graveyard: A graveyard in Nungumbakkum, Madras.

Ontikoppal: A suburb of Mysore city.

Pagade: A game of dice.

Paratha: A flatbread.

Parthasarathi Temple: Temple of Lord Krishna.

Payasam: Dessert.

Pheni: A sweet.

Poona: Now Pune, a city in Maharastra.

Prajavani: A Kannada daily.

Pulkiyogare: A dish of fried rice.

Punjabi: From Punjab; also, name of the language of Punjab, north India.

Purasavaakkam: A suburb of Madras.

Rajasthani: From Rajasthan.

Rajput warrior: Belonging to the warrior clan in Rajasthan.

Ramakrishna: Saintly nineteenth-century Bengali mystic, known to the West through the teachings of his disciple, Swami Vivekananda, who introduced Modern Hinduism to audiences abroad.

Rangoli powder: Colourful powders used to decorate the front yard and the threshold of houses.

Rasam: Lentil soup.

Rava dosa: Pancake of wheat and lentils.

Roti: unleavened bread.

Saadhwi: A chaste woman, here it is the name of a newspaper.

Sakhubai: A name.

Sambar: A south Indian vegetable stew.

Sampige (Agnoliaceae): A large tree native to India; flowers in early spring, usually along the boulevards.

Sankethi Brahmin: A Brahmin subcaste.

Sari: Main garment worn by Indian women.

Saru: Gravy.

Shree churna: A red powder worn on the forehead by orthodox brahmins of the Iyengar caste.

Sikh: Member of turban-clad sect from Punjab, north India.

Srirangam: A city in Tamil Nadu.

Sugandharaja: Creamy white flowers that bloom at night, their scent is said to attract snakes.

Supari: After-dinner mint, small pieces of areca nut.

Swami Ramanujacharya: Twelfth-century philosopher and founder of the Srivaishnava community and Iyengar caste.

Tabla: Indian musical instrument, percussion type.

Tamaram: A locality in Madras (Chennai).

Tamil: A south Indian language.

Talkadu: A town in Karnataka state, where a temple is partially submerged in sand dunes. Legend has it, the chaste Rani Rangamma, wife of a local chieftain, was violated by a member of the royal family.

Rani Rangamma cursed her ancestral town. 'Let Talkadu submerge in sand; let the Maalangi river become a muddy pool, and let the kings of Mysore become barren.' For centuries, the Mysore kings had no male heirs.

Tangi: Younger sister.

Telugu: A south Indian language spoken mostly in Andhra Pradesh.

The Hindu: English-language newspaper from Chennai.

Thiruvellikkeni: Old Tamil name for Triplicane, a suburb of Madras, where the Ranganatha Temple is located. Triplicane is the birthplace of A. K. Ramanujan's father.

Thumris: Romantic songs, classical style.

Thyagaraja: A celebrated Carnatic (south Indian) musician, who was born in Tamil Nadu in 1767. He composed more than 800 devotional songs in praise of his beloved god, Sri Rama. Most of his songs were composed in Telegu, Thyagaraja's mother tongue, and a few in Sanskrit.

Tippu Sultan: South Indian king who ruled the province of Mysore in the late eighteenth century (1782–99).

Totapuri mango tree: Mango tree that yields large fruit.

Tulsi plant: An Indian variety of basil, sacred plant; Tulsi, name of a girl.

Tumkur: A town in Karnataka.

Two annas: Old Indian currency, sixteen to a rupee.

Udaipur: A city in Rajasthan, north India.

Udipi temple: Temple in the city of Udipi, south India.

Uppittu: A south Indian dish.

Vedavyasa: Great sage/scribe who wrote the Vedas, and the Mahabharata.

Vemana: Telugu poet who lived in the fifteenth century.

Vishakhapattanam: A coastal city in the state of Andhra Pradesh.

Yenamma: A respectful way of addressing a woman.

Yenappa: A respectful way of addressing a man (see *Yenamma* for women).

Yojimbo: Famous Samurai film.